COMMUNITY INFLUENTIALS

COMMUNITY INFLUENTIALS

THE ELITES OF ATLANTA

By M. Kent Jennings

THE FREE PRESS OF GLENCOE
COLLIER-MACMILLAN LIMITED, LONDON

HM
141
J54

For information, address:
The Free Press of Glencoe
A DIVISION OF THE MACMILLAN COMPANY
THE CROWELL-COLLIER PUBLISHING COMPANY
60 Fifth Avenue, New York, New York 10011

Collier-Macmillan Canada, Ltd., Toronto, Ontario

DESIGNED BY SIDNEY SOLOMON

Library of Congress Catalog Card Number: 64-16959

TO THE MEMORY OF

MY FATHER

PREFACE

AND

ACKNOWLEDGMENTS

THIS BOOK IS about elites, community decision-making, and the interrelationship of the two in the southern metropolis of Atlanta, Georgia. It utilizes data gathered during the course of several months' field work. Although the study was prompted in part by an earlier report about Atlanta—Floyd Hunter's *Community Power Structure* (Chapel Hill: University of North Carolina Press, 1953)—it is an attempt neither to refute nor to support the controversial nature of the earlier research. Indeed, the objectives of the two investigations differ in some crucial respects. Nevertheless, fruitful comparisons may be drawn between the two studies. I have made some comparisons; readers may wish to draw still more. While the present book may be of value as a "follow-up" study, I trust that it will also be read with an eye toward the new departures and conceptualizations it contains.

Financial support for this study came from a grant to Frederic Cleaveland of the University of North Carolina from the Governmental Affairs Institute, which was, in turn, sponsoring a series of metropolitan studies underwritten by the Edgar Stern Family Fund. The Brookings Institution provided secretarial aid in the preparation of the manuscript.

I am indebted to several people who have had a hand in this enterprise. Robert Agger sparked my interest in local politics and rendered early advice on the design of the study. Marshall Goldstein, David Kovenock, and Stanley Pearl—all former fellow graduate students—did masterful work in conducting a sizable number of interviews. Donald Matthews and Richard Simpson made incisive comments on earlier drafts. Robert Wood also provided helpful suggestions on parts of the manuscript. My wife, Holly Jennings, has been a constant helpmate throughout. My greatest debt is to Frederic Cleaveland, mentor and friend; he provided careful direction at every stage of the project.

Not to be overlooked is the help of several score persons in Atlanta who gave generously of their time and thought. Many were called upon more than once, and some read portions of the manuscript. Since I cannot cite them individually, I take this opportunity to thank them in general.

I am grateful to The Free Press of Glencoe for the sure and patient hand of Estelle Whelan, who edited the manuscript, and to Ned Polsky and Martin Kessler for their apt suggestions.

While I profited greatly from all those who aided me, the responsibility for the final product is, of course, mine.

CONTENTS

LIST OF TABLES

THE STUDY OF

COMMUNITY

DECISION-MAKING*

As MODERN AMERICAN LIFE assumes an increasingly urban form, understanding the social phenomena of urban communities and the human behavior associated with them offers a distinct challenge to the social scientist. Comprehension of urban ways of life is a key to understanding curent modes of existence in general. In recent years, scholars have devoted increasing attention to the ways in which problems, issues, and projects are resolved in the local community. Although the primary object of such observation has not always been the urban community itself, these decision-making (or, as they are sometimes called, community leadership or community power-structure) studies are beginning to throw considerable light on that phase of urban community life.

The present work seeks to add to the growing body of knowledge in this research area. Specifically, the reported research is

---

*Portions of this chapter have been previously published in Bert E. Swanson, ed., *Current Trends in Comparative Community Politics* (Kansas City: Community Studies, Inc., 1962), pp. 18-30.

focused on critical aspects of political status and political roles as they are involved in community decision-making in Atlanta, Georgia, a southeastern metropolis. The study deals with actors occupying key political statuses, examines some relevant characteristics of such status-occupants, and explores their roles in community decision-making. Additionally, the report attempts to compare the findings of this study with those of past accounts. To explore the general nature of community decision-making inquiries and to outline the sources of questions and approaches that have influenced the present research are the objectives of this first chapter. In particular, the variety of approaches to the study of community decision-making is traced here.

Community Decision-Making

Initially we must define what we mean by the term "community decision-making." There are three major conceptions of community—geographical-political, process, and functional.[1] Almost without exception those engaged in the study of community decision-making have viewed the community in the geographical-political sense. Such an interpretation has developed largely because of the comparative ease of viewing a local unit of government as a community. The use of these bodies as basic census units and their prevalence as administrative units facilitate the collection of various types of information that would be difficult to obtain in less clearly defined interpretations of community. When we speak of community, we shall therefore ordinarily mean geographical-political units, imprecise as these units may be in terms of community as process or function.

The second part of the term "community decision-making," though perhaps intuitively understandable, lacks even the modest precision of the first. Peter Rossi, however, has supplied a useful working definition of decision-making in the community context. Community decisions are

. . . choices among alternative lines of action directed at affecting community-wide institutions. . . . A community decision is a choice among several modes of action which is made by an authoritative person or groups within the community institutions and of which the goals are the change or maintenance of community-wide institutions or facilities. . . . To qualify as a community decision, a choice must be made by an authoritative person or group, that is, one which either by law or by custom has the legitimate and recognized right to make the decision in question. The second specification indicates that the decision must involve community-wide institutions such as local government, locally oriented private associations and so on.[2]

Rossi maintains that this definition excludes various decisions that are not community oriented—decisions on extra-community markets or migrations, decisions by outside agencies like those of the state and national governments, and "nonauthoritative" decisions. Authoritative decisions range from voter decisions in local elections to decisions made by the boards of community organizations.

In excluding extra-community forces, Rossi does not imply that they have no impact on community decision-making; rather he attempts to limit the range of community decision-making to those subjects over which local residents have some measure of control. Nor does he claim that "nonauthoritative" decision-makers do not act as covert participants in the decision-making process. The distinction rests primarily on the basis that most decisions of wide consequence for a community are legitimated at some point in the process; Rossi does not ignore the influence that nonauthoritative actors may have on final decisions. Finally, we should notice that Rossi does not restrict community decision-making to choices made solely by government officials. Without doubt a majority of decisions with major public consequences are ultimately made by formal government decision-makers, whether they be voters, elective officials, or appointed administrators. On the other hand, decisions in the vital areas of economic expansion, social welfare, and religious life, for example, may be made by authoritative individuals who do not hold government positions.

This explication serves as a guideline for discussing studies that may be grouped under the rubric of community decision-making. To reveal the different trends of research in this area and the reference points for the present report, the studies are grouped according to five types of orientation: traditional political science, traditional sociology, interpersonal influence processes, case studies, and power structure. The categories are not, of course, mutually exclusive. Categorization is merely a device to highlight different orientations. Since there are already several thorough guides to the literature,[3] our purpose here is to characterize rather than to annotate.

Traditional Political Science and Sociology

Efforts at understanding community decision-making in political science are usually subsumed under the title "local government" or (less often) "local government and politics." The lacunae of traditional political science in this area have been thoroughly documented and criticized.[4] To a large extent, study has been dominated by an interest in party politics on the one hand and in municipal administration on the other. The studies have most often been unsystematic in design and reformist in intent.

Allan Richards describes the weaknesses of the traditional approach in this way:

Deficiencies in local government research result largely from a failure to be concerned sufficiently about relationships—relationships between legal norms and governmental practice, between forms of government and voter participation, between community structure and government policy, between the strength and practices of political parties and governmental organization, between community growth and changes in governmental and social phenomena. Through a broader and more intensive study of relationships, it may be possible to predict more accurately governmental and political behavior and, indeed, to encourage more successfully approved types of behavior.[5]

Nevertheless, the contributions dealing with party politics and with governmental institutional arrangements in municipalities are suggestive, in the first place, and serve as baseline data, in the second. They draw attention to the institution that has the prescribed function of resolving a significant cluster of community issues. In addition, some concerns of traditional political scientists have recently been receiving new and more sophisticated attention.

If political science can be accused of having been too segmental and timorous in its approach to community decision-making, traditional sociology has perhaps been too inclusive and ambitious. Lloyd Warner and his associates supplied the primary impetus for community studies in this vein.[6] They devoted primary interest to studying the "whole man" in the complete context of his socio-cultural life, usually confined to small communities. Their contributions to the knowledge of prestige stratification and class structure in American society were of signal importance. With this sort of orientation, it is not surprising that their attention to what we call community decision-making (in Rossi's sense) served a merely incidental purpose in relation to their primary attention to class structure. Their works typically contain a chapter on local politics, but the discussion is so inextricably intertwined with the larger purpose of the work that the "trees" of community decision-making are lost in the "forest" of community stratification.

The Lynds in the "Middletown" studies[7] adopted a similarly anthropological approach in examining the changing social structure in terms of occupational strata. Most subsequent sociological researches into class structure in the local community have followed lines similar to those of Warner and the Lynds. On some occasions, this approach to the community has focused on a particular institution within the cultural milieu in order to determine the relationships between that particular institution and the community's social structure. August Hollingshead's *Elmtown's Youth* is a classic example of this approach. As he indicates, "the data were collected to test the hypothesis that the social behavior of adolescents is functionally related to the position their families occupy in the community's social structure."[8] This study should not be interpreted, however, as a systematic investigation into the decision-making process; the description is merely auxiliary to the broader purpose.

Another example of the sociologists' concern with social structure in the community is Edward Digby Baltzell's thorough examination of Philadelphia's elite.[9] In this instance, there is a departure from the traditional concern with the whole culture (community), but there remains the absorption with stratification. Baltzell argues that the primary function of an upper class is to perpetuate its power whether it be in finance, manufacturing, or government. Once again, however, this argument is incidental to the main task of describing aspects of social structure, in this particular case the historical record of a certain stratum in the structure.

This brief sketch of the results of the traditional sociological approach to the community has been designed to reveal the limitations of these endeavors for a thorough understanding of community decision-making. As an approach to the problem of community stratification, it has been most valuable.

Its contribution to our knowledge of structures and functions of American community life and that of a few other cultures has been enormous. It has given emphasis to the gross cultural divisions of class, caste, and ethnic groups which characterize many community systems. It has also shown the relationship between the major institutional arrangements and these subcultural systems. Equally important has been the emphasis on examining the cultural whole, but with full recognition that only through isolation of the parts could interrelations and functions be determined.[10]

Emphasis on taxonomic principles, however, while useful for developing a body of knowledge about the social structure of the community, necessarily limits the applicability of these studies to more general community decision-making studies. On the other hand, the emphasis is extremely important for suggesting some of the underlying sources of behavior in the community. If traditional political science isolates the formal governmental and political party variables at work in the community, traditional sociology identifies the latent and manifest social structures, processes, and functions of the community.

Interpersonal Influence

The two approaches so far described reflect a predominantly institutional orientation, that is, they focus on group patterns characterized by a relatively high degree of stability, uniformity, formality, and generality centering around major social needs. Traditional political scientists are interested in such major institutions of formal government as city councils, laws and regulations, and party organizations, while traditional sociologists concentrate on a broader range of institutions including the family, church, and economic institutions, as well as government. Study of the community in terms of interpersonal influence, on the other hand, draws attention to less stable, less institutionally bound relationships.

Two of the earlier studies that were reported in detail are the "Southtown" study by Frank Stewart and the "Rovere" investigation by Robert Merton.[11] Merton's findings are especially provocative. He constructs useful typologies of local and cosmopolitan influentials and polymorphic and monomorphic influentials, illustrating the distinctions involved.

Merton adds a qualification to his study that applies equally well to Stewart's and to most other studies of this kind: that the inquiry focuses on *interpersonal* influence in the community, not influence in general. And,

even the closely related concepts of power and interpersonal influence are not identical. Men with power to affect the economic life chances of a large group may exert little interpersonal influence in other spheres: the power to withhold jobs from people may not result in directly influencing their political or associational or religious behavior.[12]

A final clarification is necessary: Merton deals with interpersonal influence in a wide range of substantive areas that do not fit our definition of community decision-making.

The Katz and Lazarsfeld study of interpersonal influence among women is important for the notion of a two-step flow of influence it introduces.[13] Other examples of the interpersonal-influence approach are the famous "Erie County" and "Elmira" studies.[14] We need only reiterate here the importance the authors attach to the determinative role of peer group or peer class as a source of influence on voting behavior in national elections. Concepts of cross pressures and reinforcement, for example, indicate the interpersonal-influence approach to individual decision-making in the community environment.

Despite its contributions to a theory of interpersonal influence, this research orientation is limited in its value for developing a theory of community decision-making. Its practitioners have commonly included behavior outside the boundaries of community issues, have looked almost exclusively at personal rather than at institutional or indirect influence, and have devoted only incidental attention to determination of important authoritative choices within the community. They have, however, demonstrated that interpersonal influence may well be crucial in the over-all process of decision-making, and they have pinpointed certain types of interpersonal influence to watch for, the conditions under which interpersonal influence becomes important, and some social correlates of interpersonal influence. Any thorough investigation of community decision-making must take into account the ubiquitous phenomenon of interpersonal influence.

Issue Studies

The first three approaches discussed are tangential, though not irrelevant, to the study of decision-making in the local community. Turning to what will be termed the issue approach (the term "case study" can be substituted), we find that a number of writings have dealt with concrete manifestations of community policy-making. To be sure, not all these studies use decision-making as their theoretical guides; nevertheless, they are in many respects more germane to our subject than the approaches already sketched. Reports of single-issue case studies are the usual products of this approach.

Most issue studies have been cast in the mold of series sponsored by the Inter-University Case Program and by the Eagleton Institute of Politics. While these studies may have considerable pedagogical and heuristic value, they typically lack the adequate conceptualization and systematic data necessary for building a thorough understanding of community decision-making.[15] There are exceptions. Leiper Freeman has provided one of the best analyses of this type in his description of the ways in which a city council chose among alternatives on a specific issue.[16] In their study of the selection of public housing sites in Chicago, Meyerson and Banfield also highlight in conceptual terms the various roles involved in the decision-making process.[17]

Some issue studies have explored specific institutions, which are not necessarily faced with designated problems but represent instead attempts by one or more communities to meet continuing social needs. Oliver Garceau's work on public libraries in the United States is a case in point.[18] Students of community organization and public health have contributed several studies showing the resolution of specific issues in a number of communities. After examining the determination of policy toward hospital-construction projects in 218 small communities, Paul

Miller concluded that those who obtained the hospitals were not the doctors, social workers, or farmers of the community. Rather, "they were the people who knew about dollars and banks and bookkeeping. They were the people who knew about the wealth, and for the most part, possessed it."[19]

Community issues often take the form of serious conflict. James Coleman provides a theoretical framework for analysis of this type of case in *Community Conflict*. The criteria for conflict situations are impacts on important areas of individuals' lives, differential impacts on people, and agreement among community leaders that action should be taken.[20] The conflict approach seems especially applicable in communities where traditions are not conducive to amicable settlement of issues and where there is considerable latent frustration with the status quo.

Although, of the alternatives presented so far, the case study or issue orientation most closely approximates a thorough approach to understanding community decision-making, it does have one notable weakness, a shortcoming almost endemic to the single case-study method.[21] Because investigators ordinarily cover only one problem or institution in the community, it is impossible to generalize about such other areas as health, housing, education, race relations, or forms of government. The procedure may yield quite satisfactory results, for specific purposes, but for those interested in authoritative decision-making in general it is less appropriate.[22]

The positive contributions of this approach, however, are considerable. First, the studies are highly suggestive of the overall process of community decision-making. If we know how a decision was reached in one policy area, we may gain insights, hunches, and comparative data about policy choices in other areas. This gain is particularly valuable when other research is being done in the same community from which the case is drawn. Second, while the notion that continued compilation of case studies from diverse sources will eventually produce a theory of community decision-making is of doubtful validity, it is possible that systematic analysis of issues and problems itself will greatly facilitate both the formulation and testing of hypotheses. This approach offers great opportunities for process analysis, which some critics have said is lacking in the approach to be described next.

The Power-Structure Approach

In contrast to the sometimes segmental, at other times too inclusive approaches cited above, the power-structure approach seeks to account for the total range of major decision-making in the community. Research of this type has commonly attempted to delineate the roles, processes, structures, and behavior associated with several areas of policy-making. Unfortunately, the phrase "power structure" has two important referents. In more popular parlance, it refers to the people and institutions that have the potential power to obtain ends they desire. Minority-group leaders and civic-organization personnel are wont to speak of manipulating the "power structure" to achieve certain goals. Used this way, the term is synonymous with "power elite." A second meaning, however, is analogous to the definition of structure in concepts like "social structure," "economic structure," and "political structure." For our present purposes, a power structure consists of all the more or less patterned elements involved in a power configuration or relationship. As we would not define "social structure" as the social elite, so there seems no apparent reason for discussing "power structure" only in terms of the power elite.

Even though the power-structure approach itself is the most recent of the five, its roots extend back to an earlier time and to other approaches, many of which have already been described. Particular recognition, however, should be paid in this case to a specific scholar, Lincoln Steffens, partly because the acknowledgment is often omitted and partly because our intellectual inheritance from his thinking has partially determined current research. Robert Daland has caught the essence of Steffens' contribution:

The outstanding work on urban politics remains, however, that of the muckraker, Lincoln Steffens. His work has been misunderstood by both friends and detractors. Our understanding of urban politics has hardly progressed beyond the point where Steffens left it. Steffens was neither a reformer nor an exposer of the depravity of bosses and machines. Rather he sought the sources of patterns of political actions which violated moral conscience. He did not find the source in the boss or in the machine. On the contrary, he found the bosses to be men of integrity and honesty and could not conceal his admiration for them. He portrayed the dual role of the boss and the machine—

guardian of the depressed and distributor of benefits to business enterprises which supported the machine. . . . Recognizing that urban
politics was changing, he foresaw, with remarkable prescience, that
the "political" boss would disappear when the "business" boss found
himself able to work better alone. . . . While later writers have contributed valuable evidence and detail to our understanding of the
mechanics of urban politics, they have not materially added to our
understanding of the mainsprings of political action in the great
metropolitan centers. Steffens saw politics as a legitimate competition
of interests in the public arena. He did not think that free men could
be "above" politics and yet retain democracy.[23]

Steffens described the power structures of his day as he saw them
in relationship to the major issues. Obviously his methods were
more those of the journalist than the rigorous social scientist;
yet his analysis, synthesis, and interpretation surpass that of many
latter-day social scientists.[24]

The web of relationships of which Steffens wrote can be
readily observed from the work of Floyd Hunter, a social scientist whose study of Atlanta, Georgia ("Regional City"),[25] has
exerted more influence than any other toward orienting the
study of community decision-making to the framework of power
structure. Steffens and Hunter both postulate the inextricable
intertwining of business and politics:

STEFFENS: What Boston suggested to me was the idea that business
and politics must be one; that it was natural, inevitable, and—possibly
—right that business should—by bribery, corruption, or—somehow get
and be the government.[26]

HUNTER: In the normal course of events the actions of the private
citizen, at least on a policy-making level of power, are almost indis-
tinguishable from those of formally designated officials. The dual relationship between government and economic operations tends to blur
into one process.[27]

Both see a pyramidal model for decision-making:

STEFFENS: In every city, as in every walk of life, there are principals and there are heelers; the principals are few; the heelers are
many. . . . So get the principals, and let them get their sheep.[28]

HUNTER: It became evident that certain men, even within the
relatively narrow range of decision leaders with whom I was dealing,

represented a top layer of personnel. . . .[29] The "little fellows" are continually moved to perform their proper tasks by those above them.[30]

Finally, their research procedures are similar:

STEFFENS (noting an approach he used whenever investigating business, politics, or reform): Say, kid, who is "it" here? . . . What I mean is, who's running the shebang? Who knows what's what and—who decides?[31]

HUNTER (describing the technique used in "Poplar Village," which was replicated in Atlanta): Place in rank order, one through ten, ten persons from each list of personnel—who in your opinion are the most influential persons in the field designated—influential from the point of view of ability to lead others.[32]

The political science profession was especially challenged by Hunter's Atlanta study, but sociologists and other academic specialists also were influenced to look at the community from the power-structure point of view. Hunter's essential statement was that a relatively small group of people—primarily big businessmen—exercised fairly general influence on the outcomes of major community problems, projects, and issues. The implicit and explicit structures, processes, and roles developed for Atlanta have served as a starting point for most subsequent studies, regardless of whether the researchers have accepted Hunter's research procedures and findings as valid.

Reactions to Hunter's and similar works[33] that followed in its wake were by no means universally enthusiastic. Kaufman and Jones signaled what was to be a rather widespread antipathy on the part of many political scientists and not a few political sociologists in their initial review of *Community Power Structure*.[34] A further series of questions was raised by Robert Dahl, Nelson Polsby, and Raymond Wolfinger.[35]

A central criticism was aimed at Hunter's nomination-attribution technique as a means of identifying influentials in the community and as a springboard for analyzing community decision-making. The point was made and continues to be made that there must be a focus on concrete forms, processes, and structures of power; issue resolution; decision-making; and so forth. Another major question was raised about the findings of monolithic (or slight variants thereof) power structures and ruling elites. The critics argued that most American communities exhibit various forms of polylithic structures and multiple, often competing elites. As of this date the battle, which involves both methodological and substantive questions, continues between the general adherents of studies in the Hunter tradition and those in opposition.[36]

But those in opposition have not been content only to criticize. A number of investigations have been carried out using different research techniques and arriving at conclusions that, on the whole, diverge from those in the Hunter tradition. Foremost among such inquiries is the New Haven research by Robert Dahl and his associates, Edward Banfield's work in Chicago, the collaborative study of Syracuse, Harry Scoble's careful investigation of Bennington, the Sayre and Kaufman volume on New York City, the multicommunity studies of Robert Agger and his colleagues, the small-community study by Vidich and Bensman, and (although outside the stream of American research) A. H. Birch's work in Glossop, England.[37] The common methodological threads running through most of these studies are the emphases on the evolution and outcomes of issues and the relations between various segments of the community as material for assessing the structure and process of power in the community. Substantively, the findings tend to reject the notions of monolithic power structures or a ruling elite and the pervasive influence of economic dominants. Instead, they show a multiplicity of powers centers and polylithic power structures, with economic dominants only one of several kinds of influential in the community. The influence roles of people in government and politics are generally rather prominent in these studies.

By inspection, we can discern the essential differences between the power-structure approach and the four already discussed. The scope of attention is larger than that of traditional political science, more specific than the traditional sociological approach, both more inclusive and exclusive than the focus on interpersonal influence, and more expansive than the single-issue or case-study analysis. If we desire a body of knowledge in a specific area of human behavior—patterns of influence in the community—the power-structure approach seems the most promising.

This selection neither rules out the contributions of other orientations nor bestows a crown of superiority on the power-structure approach. Other approaches, especially that of the single-case study, are extremely useful in understanding community decision-making. And it is indeed true that many of the research efforts in the power-structure field have not met the research standards that critics uphold. The advent of a new area of substantive inquiry, however, is inevitably beset with conceptual and procedural problems. With constant re-examination and criticism and continuing research, this approach seems most appropriate for answering some of the primary questions about community policy-making.

Before launching into this description of basic orientations to community decision-making, we made the point that these frames of reference were not mutually exclusive. This point is especially noteworthy in regard to the last approach, which typically combines a number of points of view. The research reported in the following chapters borrows from all five approaches. From traditional political science comes an interest in the impact of the formal governmental structure on community decision-making, the roles of government officials, and the importance of the electoral process. The older community sociology leads to examining the social and economic bases, characteristics, and concomitants of political decision-making and status. The lessons of interpersonal influence studies direct attention to the interpersonal relations of select actors in the decision-making structure. Case studies offer a way of determining different types of decision-making roles and variations in process. Finally, the power-structure approach suggests that we should try to assess the major dimensions of community influence and influentials over extended substantive areas. From all of these orientations, we also derive certain methodological and theoretical interests.

NOTES

1. These conceptions are briefly spelled out in Murray G. Ross, *Case Histories in Community Organizations* (New York: Harper & Row, Publishers, 1958), pp. 27-8.
2. Peter Rossi, "Community Decision-Making," *Administrative Science Quarterly*, I (March, 1957), 416-7.
3. One of the best and most recent, which deals with periodical literature, is Charles Press, *Main Street Politics* (East Lansing: Michigan State

University Press, 1962). See also Kent Jennings, "Study of Community Decision-Making," in Bert E. Swanson, ed., *Current Trends in Comparative Community Studies* (Kansas City: Community Studies, Inc., 1962), pp. 18-30.

4. See Lawrence J. R. Herson, "The Lost World of Municipal Government," *American Political Science Review*, LI (June, 1957), 330-45; Robert T. Daland, "Political Science and the Study of Urbanism," *American Political Science Review*, LI (June, 1957), 491-509; Allan R. Richards, "Local Government Research: A Partial Evaluation," *Public Administration Review*, XIV (Autumn, 1954), 271-7; Thomas H. Eliot, "Towards an Understanding of Public School Politics," *American Political Science Review*, LIII (December, 1959), 1032-51.

5. Richards, *op. cit.*, p. 277.

6. See especially W. Lloyd Warner and Paul S. Lunt, *The Social Life of a Modern Community* (New Haven: Yale University Press, 1941); Allison Davis, Burleigh B. Gardner, and Mary R. Gardner, *Deep South* (Chicago: University of Chicago Press, 1941); and W. Lloyd Warner, Wilfred C. Bailey, *et al.*, *Democracy in Jonesville* (New York: Harper & Row, Publishers, 1949).

7. See especially Robert S. Lynd and Helen M. Lynd, *Middletown in Transition* (New York: Harcourt, Brace & World, Inc., 1937).

8. August B. Hollingshead, *Elmtown's Youth* (New York: John Wiley & Sons, Inc., 1949), p. 1.

9. Edward Digby Baltzell, *Philadelphia Gentlemen* (New York: The Free Press of Glencoe, 1958).

10. Solon T. Kimball and Marion Pearsall, "Event Analysis as an Approach to Community Study," *Social Forces*, XXXIV (October, 1955), 58.

11. Frank A. Stewart, "A Sociometric Study of Influence in Southtown," *Sociometry*, X (March and September, 1947), 11-31, 273-86; Robert K. Merton, "Patterns of Influence," in Robert K. Merton, *Social Theory and Social Structure* (rev. and enlarged ed.; New York: The Free Press of Glencoe, 1957), pp. 387-415.

12. Merton, *op. cit.*, p. 419.

13. Elihu Katz and Paul F. Lazarsfeld, *Personal Influence* (New York: The Free Press of Glencoe, 1955).

14. Paul F. Lazarsfeld, Bernard Berelson, and Hazel Gaudet, *The People's Choice* (2d ed.; New York: Columbia University Press, 1955); and Bernard R. Berelson, Paul F. Lazarsfeld, and William N. McPhee, *Voting* (Chicago: University of Chicago Press, 1954).

15. For an evaluation of the case study method in public administration, see Edwin A. Bock, *et al.*, *Essays on the Case Method in Public Administration* (International Institute of Administrative Sciences, 1962).

16. J. Leiper Freeman, "A Case Study," in John C. Wahlke and Heinz Eulau, eds., *Legislative Behavior: A Reader in Theory and Research* (New York: The Free Press of Glencoe, 1959), pp. 228-37.

17. Martin Meyerson and Edward C. Banfield, *Politics, Planning, and the Public Interest* (New York: The Free Press of Glencoe, 1955).

18. Oliver Garceau, *The Public Library in the Political Process* (New York: Columbia University Press, 1949).

19. Paul Miller, *Community Health Action* (East Lansing: Michigan State University Press, 1953), pp. 133-4. See also Christopher Sower, *et al.*, *Community Involvement* (New York: The Free Press of Glencoe, 1957).

20. James Coleman, *Community Conflict* (New York: Bureau of Applied Social Research, 1955), p. 4.

21. For a theoretical discussion of the uses of the case study, see Seymour Martin Lipset, Martin Trow, and James Coleman, *Union Democracy* (New York: The Free Press of Glencoe, 1956), pp. 419-27.

22. A *series* of case studies in a single community represents one conscious attempt to overcome this limitation. This attempt is the keystone of three recent major analyses: of Chicago in Edward C. Banfield, *Political Influence* (New York: The Free Press of Glencoe, 1961); of Syracuse in Roscoe C. Martin, Frank J. Munger, *et al.*, *Decisions in Syracuse* (Bloomington: Indiana University Press, 1961); and, of New Haven in Robert A. Dahl, *Who Governs?* (New Haven: Yale University Press, 1961).

23. Daland, *op. cit.*, p. 497.

24. His acumen is best demonstrated in *The Autobiography of Lincoln Steffens* (New York: Harcourt, Brace & World, Inc., 1931).

25. Floyd Hunter, *Community Power Structure* (Chapel Hill: University of North Carolina Press, 1953).

26. Steffens, *op. cit.*, p. 606.

27. Hunter, *op. cit.*, p. 171.

28. Steffens, *op. cit.*, p. 627.

29. Hunter, *op. cit.*, p. 66.

30. *Ibid.*, p. 110.

31. Steffens, *op. cit.*, p. 403.

32. Hunter, *op. cit.*, p. 265.

33. Many of these works cited are in William Form and Delbert C. Miller, *Industry, Labor, and Community* (New York: Harper & Row, Publishers, 1960). Their number continues to grow. See, for example, Delbert C. Miller, "Town and Gown: The Power Structure of a University Town," *American Journal of Sociology*, LXVIII (January, 1963), 432-43.

34. Herbert Kaufman and Victor Jones, "The Mystery of Power," *Public Administration Review*, XIV (Summer, 1954), 205-12.

35. See, for example, Robert A. Dahl, "A Critique of the Ruling Elite Model," *American Political Science Review*, LII (June, 1958), 463-9; Nelson Polsby, "The Sociology of Community Power: A Reassessment," *Social Forces*, XXXVII (March, 1959), 232-6; and Raymond Wolfinger, "Reputation and Reality in the Study of Community Power," *American Sociological Review*, XXV (October, 1960), 636-44.

36. See, for example, William V. D'Antonio and Howard Erlich, eds., *Power and Democracy in America* (Notre Dame: University of Notre Dame Press, 1961); William V. D'Antonio and Eugene C. Erickson, "The Reputational Technique as a Measure of Community Power," *American Sociological Review*, XXVII (June, 1962), 363-76; and a colloquium by Nelson Polsby, Raymond Wolfinger, William V. D'Antonio, Howard Erlich, and Eugene C. Erickson in *American Sociological Review*, XXVII (December, 1962), 838-54. For a middle-ground approach, see Lawrence J. R. Herson, "In the Footsteps of Community Power," *American Political Science Review*, LXVI (December, 1961), 817-30.

37. Dahl, *Who Governs?*; Banfield, *op. cit.*; Martin, Munger, *et al.*, *op. cit.*; Harry Scoble, "Leadership Hierarchies and Political Issues in a New England Town," in Morris Janowitz, ed., *Community Political Systems*

(New York: The Free Press of Glencoe, 1961), pp. 117-45; Wallace S. Sayre and Herbert Kaufman, *Governing New York City* (New York: Russell Sage Foundation, 1960); Robert E. Agger, Bert E. Swanson, and Daniel Goldrich, *Comparative Community Politics* (New York: John Wiley & Sons, Inc., forthcoming); Arthur J. Vidich and Joseph Bensman, *Small Town in Mass Society* (Princeton: Princeton University Press, 1958); A. H. Birch, *Small Town Politics* (London: Oxford University Press, 1959). Dahl's work has now taken its place as a benchmark in this tradition, in much the same way that Hunter's epitomizes the other tradition.

2

METHODOLOGY

AND

RESEARCH SETTING

As we explained in the preceding chapter, there are various approaches and techniques that can be used in the study of community decision-making. A particular concern of many inquiries has suggested the specific approach and methodology employed in the present study. Portions of Chapter 1 and succeeding portions of this work reveal that much previous research has centered on specific kinds of actors in the community—on government officials, businessmen, communications personnel, minority representatives, civic organization leaders, and so forth.

This focus may also be directed at occupants of certain politically oriented status positions, the possible ways of attaining them, and the political roles associated with them. As legislative or administrative behavior is sometimes studied by focusing on select actors—officials, legislators, clientele representatives, lobbyists—so may decision-making behavior in the community be illuminated by attention to particular kinds of people. At this juncture in community studies it seems propitious, from a theoretical point of view, to attempt to provide continuity with past research by focusing on three select status-groupings in a particular community. The groupings include occupants of major economic posts in the community—*economic dominants;* those who hold positions formally designed to sanction and facilitate the exercise of influence in the community—*prescribed influentials;* and those who are perceived by significant others as being the most influential in community decision-making—*attributed influentials.* The conceptual framework that prompted concentration on these three major groupings and led to certain questions about them follows.

Major Concepts

Agreement on concepts and their usage comes slowly in the social sciences. Born in a period of critical evaluation of the uses and abuses of concepts, studies of community decision-making have received perhaps a disproportionate amount of scrutiny, especially in terms of the specification, measurement, and analysis of concepts. One of the difficulties in conceptualization in this area of inquiry stems from attempts to transfer concepts from other substantive areas. Another, as we suggested in Chapter 1, arises from the heritages of the different disciplines engaged in research. There has, therefore, been a good deal of distortion, not to mention confusion. It follows that the construction of a conceptual framework is a particularly difficult task in a project dealing with community decision-making. Yet conceptual specification is essential precisely because misunderstanding prevails. Bearing these difficulties in mind, we shall proceed to outline and discuss the major concepts relevant to this study.

Community decision-making and community issues. As defined in Chapter 1, "a community decision is a choice among several modes of action which is made by an authoritative person or group within the community institutions and of which the goals are change or maintenance of community-wide institutions or facilities."[1]

Community issues are "choices as to policy open to the authoritative decision-makers."[2] This definition permits the inclusion of even a two-alternative set of choices where one policy involves no change at all, that is, maintenance of the status quo. The present study examines a number of issues facing a single community both before and during the time of the research.

For some analytical purposes issues will be thought of as games or contests.

Political influence and political power. "Political influence" is a generic term referring to the relative impact of individuals or groupings on decisional outcomes with widespread effect on the community. According to this nominal definition, influence may be either intentional or unintentional. The latter type appears when an individual affects an outcome even though he may not have consciously been involved in the issue. It is the product of such phenomena as anticipated reactions, behavioral contagion, and referent power.[3]

Intentional attempts to exert political influence are defined here as acts of *political power*. Power has different perspectives.[4] To the extent that a person affects outcomes in accordance with his own intentions he has *positive power*. That is, to the extent that M achieves outcome X he has positive power. Power may also prevent others from accomplishing their goals—*veto power*. Preventing a change in the status quo is the usual application of veto power. To the extent that M prevents T from obtaining outcome X where X equals a change in the status quo, M has veto power. Finally, *filter power* consists of the selective exposure of certain people, facts, or points of view (summed up by the term "information") to positive- or veto-power wielders. To the extent that A regulates or manipulates information to M, who is able to achieve or prevent outcome X, he (A) has filter power. M's *ability* or *capacity* to achieve outcomes, to prevent certain outcomes, or to select information for exposure to power wielders may be considered the index of his *potential power*. The use of quantified indices and of case studies helps to reveal the protean character of power.[5] Even though unintended influence is undoubtedly a significant factor in the resolution of issues, this study concentrates primarily on intended influence (power), both because of the theoretical and methodological problems involved in the former and the concentration in this study on the relationship between political status and overt role performance.

Decision-making structure.

The term *structure* . . . means a pattern, i.e., an observable uniformity of action of operation. The general form of this concept is deliberately left in to cover a wide range of possibilities from highly stable uniformities to highly fleeting ones. This is done to avoid the problem of classification of structures and nonstructures. The various qualifications of this term enter as specific subclasses of structure. . . . Any event may contain an element indicative of a structure insofar as it is considered with regard to its nonunique aspects or characteristics.[6]

Decision-making structures may thus be highly stratified, loose, fragmented, integrated, nonintegrated, highly variable, quite permanent, and so forth. We assume here that, in the area of community decision-making, there are patterns of behavior that are amenable to empirical study; these patterns are structured, although the qualifications tell what kind of structure obtains. Analytically distinct structures may be said to exist for each community issue. The degree of similarity among these structures is a key object of analysis in this study. For convenience, the terms "political structure" and "power structure" may be substituted for decision-making structure.

Political status. To the extent that certain classes of people have different characteristics within these structures, they constitute different strata. For the most part, the present study concentrates on the elite strata. We may view these groups as having a status, the definition of status being "a position in a social group or grouping, in relation to other positions held by other individuals in the same group or grouping."[7]

There are objective and subjective ways of defining socioeconomic status; there are also alternative means of classifying *political status.* Objectively, we may arrange individuals according to the formal duties and obligations attached to certain offices they hold in politically oriented organizational units, both governmental and nongovernmental. In this sense, there are those with high political status—holders of designated important offices—and gradations from that point down to the masses, who have low status in terms of office-holding. We consider those individuals who occupy high politically oriented offices in Atlanta to have *prescribed political influence.* By this term, we mean that the formal definitions of the offices grant the incumbents a certain minimum of functions and responsibilities, which enable them to become involved in and to affect the outcomes of community issues more readily than other actors in the community's political structure.

From a subjective viewpoint, political status may be broken

down in terms of an individual's evaluation of his own status or such evaluation by others. With social class, "a person's claim to prestige and his position in the prestige hierarchy generally depend upon the way in which his behavior is evaluated by the members of his own community."[8] Similarly, political status may be based on the perceptions, evaluations, and expectations of others. People thus attribute high political status to certain individuals in a community on a nonrandom basis. Holding of an office may or may not help to determine status attribution. Individuals enjoying high political status on this basis have *attributed or perceived political influence,* our second category. We are interested in comparing these reputed influentials and the prescribed influentials.

One popular interpretation of political decision-making posits a direct relationship between high economic and high political status. This view stems from the prominence accorded to economic success in the American hierarchy of values and from economic control of vital forces in our society. Individuals in key economic positions thus have an implied, economically derived political status. The shorthand term for these people is *economic dominants.* We shall compare and contrast them with the first two groups. The analysis of political influence and decision-making in this study revolves around these three kinds of political status-groups.[9] Because they have preferred status, these groups are also referred to as *elites.*

Social status characteristics. Certain social features are traditionally associated with particular statuses. We examine the importance of these characteristics for the different kinds of political statuses.

Political roles. Accompanying political status within the decision-making structure are political roles. "Role" refers here to both the expectations and behavior accompanying particular positions, with emphasis on the latter. Whether certain role-behaviors accompany a given status is subjected to empirical inquiry and verification later. We shall also observe role-enactments as they correspond to various stages of issue resolution.

Some role-enactments may be more oriented to power acts and participation in community decision-making than are others. Such orientation is called *politicization.* In this book, we shall investigate the relative states of politicization among status-occupants and deal with the relationship between political status and the forms of influence and power already described.

The politicized roles of some status-occupants seem to be more extensive than for others. *Scope* refers to the range of issues over which actors try to or do gain favorable outcomes. Actors engaged in a limited number of issues have low scopes, while those in larger numbers have high scopes.

Status and role acquisition. How actors come to play their roles comes under our surveillance. *Political socialization* deals with the ways in which people become interested in and learn to play decision-making roles in the community. Here the method by which an individual is first introduced into a political role is especially significant. The possibilities of the status and role *sequences* are also explored.

While the major emphasis of this endeavor is on pursuing the relationship between select political actors and political roles in one community, three by-products will also emerge. First, an approximation of the over-all structure of power may be drawn. This study does not propose to describe categorically the power structure of Atlanta. But it does seem probable that a considerable number of insights may be gained, and, while a complete picture cannot be painted, perhaps a number of partial images can be accepted or rejected. Second and related to the first point, the procedures employed provide data with which to retest some of the major conclusions reported by Hunter in his earlier study: the existence of a ruling elite, the influence of economic dominants, and the weak and secondary influence of government officials. Third, there is an underlying concern with methodology and the various approaches to community decision-making studies that can perhaps shed some light on profitable avenues of study in this research area.

Research Procedures

After perusal of the customary written sources, a number of informal, exploratory interviews were held with approximately forty strategically located individuals in Atlanta.[10] These people were strategically located in the sense that they occupied certain sensitive official positions in governmental or civic bodies. Not only did these interviews prove useful for marking out the boundaries of later work, but they also produced descriptive accounts of the way certain problems were being handled and the major people and organizations involved in the issues. The combination of materials from these interviews with clues from the written sources set the stage for planning the main phase of the study.

The next step was to interview twenty key informants (some of whom had been previously interviewed) and to ask them for nominations of those whom they considered to be most influential in making community decisions with wide consequences for the community as a whole. The fifty-nine people who garnered 90% of the 416 nominations constituted the operationally defined *attributed influentials* at this stage. From the written materials and informal interviews, we had already accumulated a roster of major actors involved in a number of current or recent community issues. It is worth noting that at least half of the nominated people were included in this earlier list.

Government officials, both appointive and elective, are generally considered the top formal decision-makers in the governmental sphere. We compiled a list of the major governmental officials in the city and in Fulton County. The criteria for inclusion in this list were the substantive concern of the official, salary level, and formal authority vested in the office. Of the forty people who met these standards, fifteen had been included in the attributed influentials, so that the final total of government officials was twenty-five, and they were added to the list.

Norton Long, among others, has emphasized the key role that civic-staff people may play in community policy-making. "The staff man in the civic field is the typical protagonist of things in general—a kind of entrepreneur of ideas. . . . Civic staff men, ranging from chamber of commerce personnel to college professors and newspapermen, are in varying degrees interchangeable, and provide an important network of communication."[11] The exploratory work had shown at least the partial validity of this formulation before Long's article appeared. Great reliance was placed upon the earlier work in compiling a list of twenty-five nongovernmental staff people, half of whom were paid and the remainder either semi-professional leaders of various specialized civic organizations or people previously identified as playing predominantly staff roles. Subtracting three people who had already qualified for the nominations list left twenty-two civic-staff personnel. Coupled with the government officials they composed the *prescribed inflentials*.

The composition of the final classification was guided by

the preoccupation of a number of researchers with the dominance in local decision-making processes of the economic elite of the community. Using a technique adapted from an earlier study,[12] forty-one *economic dominants* were singled out. The criteria employed were that the person must either be the top executive of a local firm or branch office of 700 or more employees, be then serving on the boards of directors of three or more locally centered firms, or be the top executive of one of the five leading financial (banking) units in the area. Although some individuals qualified on the basis of two or more of these criteria, approximately four-fifths of them were included solely because of their executive positions in local firms or branch offices.[13] Fourteen of these economic dominants had qualified under the nomination procedures, so that a balance of twenty-seven remained to bring the total list of all status-occupants to 133. One hundred nineteen (89%) of them were subsequently interviewed on the basis of a standardized questionnaire.[14] Nearly one-half were also interviewed in a more informal fashion.

During the standardized interviews, the respondents were asked to designate the fifteen most influential people in the list of 133. Once again, using 90% of the total vote cast as a cutoff point, fifty-seven individuals were defined as *attributed influentials*. Fifty-seven of the fifty-nine who had originally been attributed with high influence were similarly recognized by this much broader, more inclusive universe.[15] The other groups then consisted of forty-seven prescribed influentials and twenty-nine economic dominants.

Actually, the attributed influentials list is sometimes divided into first- and second-levels for purposes of this analysis. It seems plausible to assume that certain characteristics may be associated with a person's rank in terms of perceived influence. By comparing the two levels of attributed influentials on a number of factors, this assumption can be tested.[16] The prescribed influentials were also divided for particular analytical purposes. While the government officials and the civic-staff people do have some marked similarities, they diverge on other matters.

One further point is in order. As apparent from the description of how the members of each status-group were determined, our research was particularly concerned with the attributed influentials, for both methodological and empirical reasons. The attributed influentials are *the* reputed power elite of the community; they therefore provide an excellent grouping for testing a number of assertions that have been made about community decision-making in Atlanta, as well as in other communities. That is why the government officials and economic dominants who are also members of the attributed elite will be analyzed primarily as members of that elite. In the comparisons between elites, they will not be "counted twice." At various points, however, we will indicate some characteristics and behavior patterns of those persons who are, technically, members of more than one elite.

The Atlanta Area

Various characteristics of a community impinge upon and vitally affect roles and statuses in the decision-making process. In large part, they are those features that make for differences in power structures from community to community. While this section is by no means an exhaustive catalog of community variables that can shape the decision-making behavior of political actors, it does suggest some major conditioning factors and outlines some of the main environmental forces that may be important for any given issue.

Physical outline. Mid-twentieth-century Atlanta is a dynamic metropolis of about one-half million people within the city limits and another one-half million in the five-county standard metropolitan statistical area. From a physical point of view, Atlanta has had little to block its expansion either in terms of geographical barriers or political boundaries. Since its largest growth occurred after the advent of the automobile, its population has pushed outward rather than upward. The central city did not have to absorb the population growth that many older cities did. Subsequently, however, the city boundaries have been extended to include part of the outward growth. Almost 90% of the city's half-million population lies within Fulton County, with the balance in DeKalb County. Atlanta accounts for about three-fourths of Fulton County's population. The relative dispersion of the Atlanta-area population is indicated by the fact that between 1950 and 1960 Fulton County suffered a net migration loss of almost 2000 people, while the five-county standard metropolitan statistical area gained nearly 130,000.

Governmental and partisanship structure. The municipal government of Atlanta is classified formally as a weak mayor-council type. Only recently has the mayor gained the authority to appoint a majority of the department heads (as the incumbents retire or die), subject to approval of the board of aldermen. Aldermen are elected at large but must reside in the wards they represent. A consequence of this arrangement is the practice of "ward courtesy," a custom tending to inhibit systematic policy-making and execution by the city government. The board of education is also elected at large, and its eight members must also live in the wards they represent. Eight lay boards serve the city. As a rule of thumb, we would expect ward representation, when coupled with weak formal mayoralty powers and a number of lay boards, to inhibit strong leadership. Yet Mayor William H. Hartsfield, who held office over twenty years, attained a reputation for having overcome these difficulties on many occasions.

Fulton County's major governing body is a three-man commission elected at large within the entire county. The chairmanship tends to rotate on the commission; leadership quality traditionally varies with the occupancy of the chairmanship. Fulton County is one of the few southern counties with a county manager. By design and in practice his power is limited. Four citizen boards serve the county. Additionally, seven lay boards serve both the city and county. Under the Plan of Improvement adopted in 1951, the city performs certain services for the entire county, while the county has exclusive jurisdiction in a smaller number of substantive areas. A few functions like education are still carried out separately by the two jurisdictions. Unlike Atlanta, Fulton County's board of education is appointed by the grand jury. Outside analysts rate the general performance of the governments of Atlanta and Fulton County as better than average.

Problems of metropolitan fragmentation have perhaps been smaller in Atlanta than in most other American metropolises, in large part because of the adoption of the Plan of Improvement and practices like the joint city-county lay boards. A vigorous Metropolitan Planning Commission, which has now been expanded to include the five-county standard metropolitan statistical area, has also proved useful in promoting intergovernmental integration. Situated as it is geographically, the Atlanta metropolitan area is not beset with interstate strains in solving its problems. Finally, Atlanta and Fulton County are so much the hub of the metropolis that decisions affecting them tend to set the tone for the entire area.

Two-party politics is nonexistent in Atlanta city elections. Nor does there appear to be any of the stable multifactionalism that sometimes gives southern politics a semblance of partisanship. While he held office, Mayor Hartsfield had something of a personal machine—opposition was usually poorly organized and episodic. During his terms, Hartsfield encouraged a number of present aldermen to run for office. In the county, the factional alignments are even more loosely structured.

A final point is that Atlanta, as a single metropolis in a predominantly rural state, conforms to a customary pattern of deviation from the remainder of the state in electoral behavior. For example, although Georgia as a whole gave approximately seven-tenths of its votes to Adlai Stevenson in 1956, only slightly more than one-half of the Fulton County voters did so. Comparable proportions for John F. Kennedy in 1960 were about three-fifths and one-half. In 1962, electors in the fifth congressional district, dominated by populous Fulton and DeKalb Counties, cast 45% of their ballots for a Republican candidate after earlier defeating the conservative Democrat James Davis in the noncounty unit primaries. The same balloting witnessed election of a Republican state senator from the city's "silk-stocking" district. Finally, Atlanta and its environs traditionally vote for the more "liberal" Democratic candidates in statewide primaries.

The popular impression is that Atlanta and its environs are discriminated against by the state legislature because of the suspect character of Atlanta's attitudes on major political, social, and economic questions of the day. For example, in comparison with other leading southern cities, Atlanta ranked low in the late 1950's in the relative amount of state aid received for both school and city government purposes. While Georgia received more than 20% of its total state taxes from Atlanta and returned only approximately 5% in state aid, it refused to allow Atlanta to expand its own taxing facilities.

Economic features. Economic balance is at the moment a keynote of Atlanta's economy. The area's economic destiny was charted mainly on the basis of its position as a transportation center. It is now a rapidly expanding metropolis, serving as southern regional headquarters for a number of corporate and governmental establishments. In addition, it has a great variety of home-owned firms engaged in manufacturing, as well as commerce, finance, and service. Since the end of World War II, a number of large manufacturing plants, including some in the automotive and air industries, have located in the area. Nevertheless, in 1960 manufacturing accounted for only about one-fifth of the employment of the Atlanta urbanized area, while retail and wholesale trade activities accounted for slightly more than another one-fifth.[17] Diversification of its economic activities has provided long-run economic stability for the community as a whole. On the civic front, such Atlanta-based firms as Rich's, Georgia Trust, First National Bank, Southern Bell, Georgia Power, and Coca-Cola have a long tradition of involvement in community decision-making.

Civic associations. The civic organization structure in Atlanta has three main groupings.[18] One is dominated by the mature Chamber of Commerce, an organization of approximately 2000 firms and a staff of over twenty. Many people in Atlanta speak of the Chamber as a sun around which many of the lesser organizations, called satellites, revolve. The Chamber's wide-ranging major policy statements are usually prepared by a committee headed by a prominent lay member assisted by a professional. Although the association occasionally becomes involved in controversial community issues, for the most part it avoids topics that challenge the basic institutional arrangements of the community until it is sure of the outcome.

The most prominent of the satellites is the Central Atlanta Association. Its membership numbers around 150, including both individuals and firms. A rather elite group, the strategy of this organization rests upon the presumption that the prestige of the membership will carry most policies they favor. As the executive secretary puts it, "We have the men, not the boys." Virtually all the members of this association are also members of the Chamber. Another satellite is the Traffic and Safety Council. For some years it was attached to the Chamber but now has independent status. This organization of 500 or more members plays a watchdog and initiating role in traffic developments in Atlanta. Several major traffic ordinances of the past few years have originated from its staff.

There are, of course, other civic organizations in this grouping, but most of them are minor compared with these three. They exist mainly to serve an overseer's function and to promote programs largely confined to business affairs. While the luncheon clubs are an essentially different type of organization, they are included in this cluster too. In a city with well-staffed civic organizations to handle substantive matters, on the one hand, and numerous social clubs to fill social needs, on the other, the importance of the service clubs appears to be minimal.[19]

This cluster of civic organizations might be termed the business-civic type. A second variety includes what could be called the good government-civic type. Traditionally, such continuing organizations are dominated by women, with some men drawn from the various professions, as is the case in Atlanta. Voting organizations and school-related associations are the primary types in this category. While the League of Women Voters and the Atlanta Voters Guild specialize in monitoring and publicizing the truly public manifestations of local government, the school-oriented bodies both monitor and promote. As a device for imposing restraints on unauthorized conduct and for promoting the cause of "good government," the voting organizations are not unimportant in Atlanta. Their excellent relations with the mass-media personnel, who regard them as unbiased organizations, help in this respect. As for the educational organizations, represented primarily by the Parent-Teachers Association Council, their city-wide organizations provide support for school administrative officials. On the surface, at least, it appears that the Council and its subsidiaries had been co-opted by the educational officials for a number of years, so that its role as critic had been minimized. Nevertheless, for gaining grass roots support, they were and remain vitally important, especially in the absence of political-party organizations.

A third cluster of civic organizations is found in the private welfare field. For the most part a certain affluence or access to resources is necessary for top-level lay involvement in such programs on a community-wide basis. In private welfare activities, Atlanta has a super-organization—the United Appeal—and a host of specialized agencies for which the United Appeal gathers money and performs certain housekeeping services. There are, however, major independent organizations too. Resembling the welfare bodies in their emphasis on economic resources are the cultural organizations. Empirically, there is a moderate amount of overlap between the cultural and welfare fields in the participation of lay leaders. For the three hierarchies as a whole, there is much more overlap within and between the business-civic type and the welfare type than any other combination. The women's organizations are rather isolated.[20]

Minority groups. We have occasion to refer throughout this work to minority representatives and their roles. A general introduction will place the minorities in perspective. Slightly more than one-third of Atlanta's population is Negro. The Negro community is highly developed economically, socially, and politically. In the economic sphere, it is a showplace of Negro accomplishment, a source of pride to both whites and Negroes in the community. Relatively good economic conditions have fostered many middle- and upper-class residential areas, social clubs, and a well defined status hierarchy. There are at least two main social groups—one associated with the higher educational institutions and one oriented to business.

Politically, a voting organization known as the Atlanta Negro Voters League has transformed the Negro vote into a potential bloc that at times does indeed vote *en masse,* while splitting its votes at other times. In city elections, a screening board of the organization interviews (interrogates may not be too strong a word) virtually all prospective candidates. Before election day, endorsement of a slate of candidates is announced informally and often formally as well. The organization's batting average, particularly in Atlanta mayoralty contests, is high.

Even though Negroes may help to elect favorable candidates, they themselves are seldom found on top policy-making boards in the community, whether they be governmental boards or interest groups. Although the Negro has more political influence in Atlanta than in many communities in both North and South, the differences in the white man's world and the Negro's are still highly visible. They continue to be sources of frustration and potential social and political conflict between the two races. One indicator of this problem is the rather strong student protest movement.[21] Another is a pamphlet called "A Second Look: The Negro Citizen in Atlanta," an incisive indictment by the "Young Turk" Atlanta Committee for Cooperative Action.

Another minority element has not prospered so well relative to the Negroes. Even when compared to other southern states, labor in Georgia is relatively unorganized. In the standard metropolitan area of Atlanta, optimistic figures show that 20% of the nonagricultural labor force is unionized. The conservative guess is 10%. If the real figure lies roughly halfway between the two estimates, unionized labor constitutes about 15% of the employed. The industrial unions claim roughly one and one-half times more members than do the craft unions. The largest single block of organized workers is found in the United Auto Workers, with approximately 7000 members (as of the late 1950's).

Judging from the data gathered in this investigation, labor is neither so well organized politically as the Negro community nor so politically involved. But the climate for organized labor is not necessarily hostile. Without intensive investigation of labor's political role in Atlanta, we would nevertheless conclude that, as in many nonsouthern cities where labor is only mildly influential,[22] labor has not been fully integrated into the decision-making complex of the community.

A distinctly successful and quite prominent minority element in Atlanta is the Jewish community (here community is used in the sense of process or function), whose members form approximately 5% of the area's population. As we shall see later, leading Jews have not only succeeded financially but have also become high-level participants in the policy-making process. The older Jewish families, immigrants from Germany, are gradually giving way to the leadership of more recent arrivals from Eastern Europe. As in most communities throughout the United States, Jewish people are still denied access to the social clubs of the Gentile world. There is little, if any, Jewish political organization as such, but the social organizations are numerous and well staffed. In terms of the Jewish community's elite, it is possible to identify a theological elite, an organizational elite dominated by the professionals, and a lay elite.[23]

The press. Atlanta denizens are exposed to a variety of mass media designed for local consumption. Although the impact of television and radio may be greater, the role of the press is still regarded as more crucial in local issues. In part, this view stems from the editorializing in which the press can engage, while the broadcasters are more constrained. As is increasingly the case in American cities, Atlanta and its environs are served by jointly owned morning and evening papers. Both papers have served as convenient whipping boys for Georgia politicians vying for statewide offices. For historical and socio-economic reasons, the morning *Atlanta Constitution* tends to circulate more among the Negroes and the upper-middle and upper social classes, while the afternoon *Atlanta Journal* draws its readership from the broad range of the middle and lower white classes. For some years, the existence of these different audiences helped to explain the main editorial difference between the two papers in regard to local issues. Against the *Journal's* more conservative statements on racial problems stood the *Constitution's* moderate-to-liberal opinions. To a great extent the *Constitution,* under Ralph McGill's editorship, came to be a rallying point for the less conservative on this issue. In very recent years, however, the *Journal* has dropped its more conservative posture.

Although their positions on other issues ordinarily do not differ a great deal, selective coverage and emphasis do serve to maintain a moderate amount of competition between the two papers at the reportorial level. Neither paper is a captive of local officials. The top executives of the enterprise tend to become highly involved in local issues, both behind the scenes and in overt fashion. The papers are inclined to vary their strategy in regard to pushing public issues. For example, in one mayoralty election, they declared for Hartsfield early and loudly, while in another they waited until just before election time to voice their backing for Hartsfield, even though they had long since made their choice.

In addition to the two leading papers, a number of minor papers, including the *Atlanta Daily World* (a Negro publication) and several suburban publications, serve the area. Aside from the Negroes themselves, only those whites whose daily work involves policy-oriented behavior toward the Negro community make a practice of reading the *Daily World.* At times, the suburban presses challenge the stands of the two large dailies, especially over issues involving increased expenditures. Only on rare occasions, however, does their opposition prevail. Their circulation is not wide.

Cosmopolitanism. Atlanta has a cosmopolitan atmosphere, a phenomenon that seems to influence the conduct of public life in the community. Institutions of higher education, governmental regional offices, cultural activities, branch offices of major corporations, and the feeling and fact of being a regional headquarters in varied social and economic activities contribute to this cosmopolitanism. Associating and identifying with worldly affairs may well temper the latent tendencies in southern politics toward demagoguery, prejudice against minorities, and resort to violence among political influentials. This cosmopolitanism —perhaps ideology is not too strong a word—seems to have been a factor, for example, in facilitating the desegregation of Atlanta schools in 1961.

The primary objectives of our field research may now be spelled out in summary form as they will be presented in the ensuing chapters. Chapter 3 deals with relevant social characteristics associated with the status-holders, with the objective of exploring the relationships between social traits and political status. Chapter 4 presents a gross picture of the politicization of the actors under study. It seeks to show, in a general fashion, rates and types of politicization and to explore why these factors may vary among the different status-groups. The objective of Chapter 5 is to see how extensive the roles of the various actors are in terms of substantive areas. Is role-scope associated with political status, and what does the answer tell us about the configuration of power in Atlanta? To investigate more fully the political role-enactments associated with different statuses is the aim of Chapters 6 and 7. Looking at specific roles and types of power in terms of stages of community policy-making adds graphic data for relating status and role, as well as for depicting ways of policy-making in Atlanta. In Chapter 8, we confront the questions whether Atlanta is dominated by a ruling elite and to what extent the economic notables are the community's "real" decision-makers. Chapter 9 is an exploratory examination of how political statuses and roles come to be acquired. It also chronicles some devices and structures through which these statuses and roles are maintained. Finally, Chapter 10 attempts an interpretive summary of the entire study in its substantive and theoretical aspects.

NOTES

1. Peter Rossi, "Community Decision-Making," *Administrative Science Quarterly*, I (March, 1957), 416.

2. *Ibid.*, p. 417.

3. Anticipated reactions are discussed in Carl J. Friedrich, *Constitutional Government and Democracy: Theory and Practice in Europe and America* (Boston: Ginn & Company, 1946), pp. 589-91; behavioral contagion by

Norman Polansky, Ronald Lippit, and Fritz Redl in "An Investigation of Behavioral Contagion in Groups," *Human Relations*, III (1950), 319-48; and referent power by John R. P. French, Jr., and Bertram Raven, "The Bases of Social Power," in Dorin Cartwright, ed., *Studies in Social Power* (Ann Arbor: The University of Michigan Press, 1959), pp. 150-67.

4. The following discussion borrows from Edward A. Suchman, John P. Dean, and Robin M. Williams, Jr., *Desegregation: Some Propositions and Research Suggestions* (New York: Anti-Defamation League of B'nai B'rith, 1958), pp. 21-4.

5. This discussion of influence and power is, of course, not a full explication of the terms. The definitions offered do, however, provide a framework for analyzing the types of behavior that fall under the major aims of the study. For theoretical discussions of power and influence, with especial emphasis on the difficulties of precise measurement, see James G. March, "Concepts in the Theory of Influence," *Journal of Politics*, XIX (May, 1957), 202-26; his "An Introduction to the Theory and Measurement of Influence," *American Political Science Review*, XLIX (June, 1955), 431-51; Robert A. Dahl, "The Concept of Power," *Behavioral Science*, II (July, 1957), 201-15; Felix E. Oppenheim, "Degrees of Power and Freedom," *American Political Science Review*, LIV (June, 1960), 437-46; Harold Lasswell and Abraham Kaplan, *Power and Society* (New Haven: Yale University Press, 1950), especially pp. 71-6; Herbert Goldhamer and E. A. Shils, "Types of Power and Status," *American Journal of Sociology*, XLV (September, 1939), 171-82; and Dorin Cartwright, *op. cit.*

6. Marion J. Levy, *Structure of Society* (Princeton: Princeton University Press, 1952), pp. 57-8.

7. Arnold W. Green, *Sociology: An Analysis of Life in Modern Society* (New York: McGraw-Hill Book Co., Inc., 1956), p. 37.

8. Kurt B. Mayer, *Class and Society*, "Doubleday Short Studies in Sociology" (Garden City: Doubleday & Company, Inc., 1955), p. 24.

9. "Political status" is defined and used in a different fashion in Robert E. Agger, et al., "Political Influence Structures," in Bert E. Swanson, ed., *Current Trends in Comparative Community Studies* (Kansas City: Community Studies, Inc., 1962), pp. 81-8.

10. The author and Prof. Frederic N. Cleaveland of the Department of Political Science, University of North Carolina, conducted these interviews during the summer and fall of 1957.

11. Norton E. Long, "The Local Community as an Ecology of Games," *American Journal of Sociology*, LXIV (November, 1958), 258-9.

12. Robert O. Schulze and Leonard U. Blumberg, "The Determination of Local Power Elites," *American Journal of Sociology*, LXIII (November, 1957), 292.

13. Robert A. Dahl cites some of the literature that suggests the greater importance of executives *vis à vis* directors in "Business and Politics: A Critical Appraisal of Political Science," *American Political Science Review*, LIII (March, 1959), especially p. 309. See also James Burnham, *The Managerial Revolution* (New York: The John Day Company, Inc., 1941); and David T. Bazelon, "Facts and Fictions of U. S. Capitalism," *The Reporter*, September 17, 1959, pp. 43-8. Both because most directors of national firms do not live in the community under investigation and because it seems that,

on the local scene at least, an economic firm's participation in community life is largely conducted by executives, the criterion for directors to be included on the list was made more stringent than those for executives.

14. These interviews were carried out in a period beginning in the late summer of 1958 and extending into the spring of 1959. This writer conducted approximately two-thirds of the interviews. They ranged in time from fifty minutes to more than three hours, with the average being close to one hour and a half. Outright refusals, sickness, and job transfers accounted for the 11% not interviewed.

15. Agreement among the three principal status-groups as to the composition of the attributed influentials group was high. Even though the attribution rank of a particular individual might vary from one grouping to another, near unanimity emerged on the total composition of this particular population. Greatest consensus existed among the status-groups on the twenty or so people who received the most designations as influentials.

16. To distinguish analytically between these two strata, a compromise between two measures was used. Taking the total number of nominations cast for the fifty-seven persons as 100%, we wanted to divide the perceived influentials as close to the median as possible. On the other hand, we looked for a "natural break" that would show a major distinction in the respondents' designations. The compromise resulted in classifying the twenty-three individuals who received 56% of all votes as first-level and the remainder as second-level attributed influentials.

17. In the classification developed by Reiss and Duncan, Atlanta, in relation to other cities of the same size (in 1950), had a high per capita value of sales in both wholesale and retail trade and the metropolitan area had a relatively high position in wholesale trade. The economic-base theory rests primarily on the relative amount of a commodity "exported" from the community. A functional specialization in wholesale and retail trade is thus based on the relative amount of trade exported. The city also had a minor specialization in education, which means figuratively that it exported education. See Otis Dudley Duncan and Albert J. Reiss, Jr., *Social Characteristics of Urban and Rural Communities* (New York: John Wiley & Sons. Inc., 1956). For more recent comparisons, see "Atlanta Silhouettes: People, Jobs, and Land" (Atlanta: Atlanta Region Metropolitan Planning Commission, 1962).

18. The civic association is to the local community what trade, labor, agricultural, and other types of association are to the nation as a whole. As their title implies, however, the civic organizations are often viewed as more selfless than their national counterparts. They are more often looked upon as playing integrative, rather than fragmentive, roles. Then, too, civic associations are usually of the trade variety, rather than agricultural or labor, in most American communities. For our purposes, a civic organization is defined as a nongovernmental body of a voluntary or nonprofit nature that includes among its major goals the influencing of community decisions. This goal frequently requires making claims through or upon local government agencies and these associations are therefore political interest groups in the same sense as associations at the state and national levels.

19. Some data suggest that the smaller the community the more nearly service clubs approach the role of the civic organizations in a larger com-

munity. Note Oliver Garceau's comment in *The Public Library in the Political Process:* "From the experience of our survey, the influence of the service clubs in cities under 200,000 population would seem to be greater than has been generally recognized. The libraries have found them of great value in reaching that group of influential men who do not use the library, but are important in community opinion and political action." (New York: Columbia University Press, 1949), p. 114.

20. Although they are of some importance in community decision-making, such aspects of community life as health organizations, church and religious organizations, and cultural and educational institutions have not been described in detail because of space limitations and because they do not bear directly on this study.

21. Primary research for this study antedated the "sit-ins" and other forms of social protest registered by young Negroes throughout the South, including Atlanta. The demonstrations appear to be exerting a profound effect on the political structure of Atlanta's Negro community, as well as of the community at large. For more details, see Jack L. Walker, "Protest and Negotiation: A Case Study of Negro Leadership in Atlanta, Georgia," *Midwest Journal of Political Science,* VII (May, 1963), 99-124.

22. For an account of several studies showing labor's place in the community power structure, see William Form and Delbert C. Miller, *Industry, Labor, and Community* (New York: Harper & Row, Publishers, 1960).

23. Some of these statements are based on Solomon Sutker, "The Jews of Atlanta: Their Social Structure and Leadership Pattern" (unpublished M.A. thesis, University of North Carolina, 1950).

3

SOCIAL BACKGROUNDS,

SOCIAL CHARACTERISTICS,

AND POLITICAL STATUS

THE ATTAINMENT OF various types of political status is no matter of chance, Donald Matthews has shown in résumé form that formal political decision-makers at various levels and in different countries have widely disparate social backgrounds from those of the average individuals in the same societies.[1] Community decision-making studies using the reputational approach usually present the social characteristics of the perceived elite.[2] Both in terms of social backgrounds and present social characteristics, holders of preferred political statuses may be expected to diverge not only from the general public but also, perhaps, from one another.

In this chapter, then, we examine some relevant data on the broadly defined social backgrounds and contemporary characteristics of the three elites—attributed (perceived) influentials, prescribed influentials, and economic dominants. We investigate both background data and present features that help to distinguish and characterize the elites. We do not mean to say that a causal relationship necessarily exists between possessing a cer-

38

tain feature and holding a particular status, but it is evident
that a given trait may be highly associated with a given status
in some instances and very little in others. All people with
quality A may not be of status X, but people of status X may
almost invariably possess quality A.[3] In this sense, A is a correlate
(and perhaps a requisite) of X. It should be noted that the
focus of this chapter is not on the inferred behavioral consequences of various social indices.

Ascribed Social Status

Some determinative social characteristics are vested in the
individual at an early stage in his life. They are generally ex-
ternal factors over which he has no control. Such bequests are
often matters of social-status ascription.

Race and sex. In Atlanta, as in most American communities, higher political (and economic) status is accorded members
of the white race and the male sex. Although Negroes form
one-third of the population of Atlanta, they constitute well under
10% of the attributed and prescribed political influentials and
account for none of the economic dominants. One of the two
Negro perceived influentials is a lawyer who has been instrumental in leading Negro voting organizations at the local and
state levels. His role as a pivotal man in city and county elections is widely recognized by both whites and Negroes. The
second Negro is the president of an eminently successful financial
institution. His success in his business has opened the way for
more communication between the Negro and white communities
in the fields of finance and business than would have been
possible otherwise. He is also a potent figure in local and state
elections.

Two of the four Negroes with prescribed influence are staff
members of the Atlanta Urban League. Because of their technical expertise and continual attention to community problems,
these two hold positions of respect in the Negro community,
and they also serve as a channel for transmitting information
to and from the white community. The other two prescribed
influentials are both extremely active as leaders in Negro organizations and committees. One is the president of one of Atlanta's
excellent Negro colleges, while the other has made his mark in
a fashionable real-estate and insurance business. The latter made

an unsuccessful but strong bid for a seat on the aldermanic board in 1957. More recently, he was the losing candidate in a contest for a state senate seat. The victor, however, was also a Negro.

From these cases we can conclude that it is probably easiest for Negroes to gain high political status on the strength of their leadership in strong organizations and institutions. In a community where the major institutions are racially segregated, this leadership is necessarily in Negro organizations. But it is also important that these organizational leaders be in a position to communicate with other organizational and institutional representatives in the community at large.

Since men rather than women customarily occupy the major economic and governmental posts in a community, it is not surprising that women account for so few of the status-occupants. Where women do participate in community decision-making, their tendency is to act in a supporting or auxiliary role or to concentrate on a specialized arena particularly conducive to lay participation. As Sower comments, "community action, especially that which is related to health, welfare or children and which requires time and effort over and above the determination or administration of the financial resources of a community, frequently mobilizes the active women of the locality."[4]

This pattern applies to the seven women who qualify for elite status in our study. Only one woman—the prominent superintendent of the city school system—ranked as an attributed influential.[5] She won this status primarily because of the respect engendered by her administration of the school system. She was eminently successful in co-opting the school-related organizations of the community, and her one-time involvement in state politics also contributed to her high status.

Two of the six women in the prescribed elite are nonprofessionals who, at the time of the study, exercised leadership roles in the League of Women Voters and the Atlanta Voters Guild. These organizations, by monitoring the formal governmental process, attempt to affect policy-making, but they seldom actually make policy decisions. A third woman headed the city-wide Parent Teachers Association. Another presided over the election committee of the city, while a fifth exercised leadership in the area of human relations. The remaining member had extensive contacts in the community, being involved in electoral, civic, and charitable activities in addition to serving in the communications field, where she concentrates on community developments.

Two of the seven women, then, are connected with educational matters, three with the electoral process, one with human relations, and one with a variety of areas. Professionalization seems to offer the best opportunity for attributed influence in the community, but it is not necessarily required for prescriptive influence.

Age. Another variable over which an individual has no control is age. How important is age for attaining membership in a political elite? Mature age is most significantly associated with the attributed influentials, 60% of them being over fifty-five. Three explanations are suggested. In the first place, older age may in itself arouse deference and accordance of prestige to an individual. A certain myth about superior knowledge and wisdom accumulated over the years often leads people to respect the elder citizens of a community, who are thus accorded high political status. Second, higher visibility and publicity are usually tendered to older people, and greater opportunities for recognition may result in higher status.

Another, and more likely, explanation is that, up to a point, the older one grows the higher the institutional position he is likely to hold. Company executives, chairmen of the board, and ranking public officials are usually selected from older age brackets. If the presidency of a company or the chairmanship of an important aldermanic committee is considered a key political post in the community decision-making process, then its occupant will have high political status, and age may thus be a conditional factor.

An example from Atlanta illustrates the point. One of the perceived influentials had recently been named president of a large service industry active in most of the South. As a vice-president, he had had little to do with community affairs, since he was away from the community a great deal. A tradition of involvement in Atlanta policy-making is, however, associated with the presidency of this firm. Immediately upon assuming office, he was named to help head one of the large-scale charity drives in the community as a first step toward entering the decision-making structure. He also became involved in a number of public issues then under discussion in the community. Although it was his career position that really accounted for his involvement, without his mature age and years of experience with the company, he would not have secured that position.

Another illustration concerns an individual who had recently been elevated to the chairmanship of his board. In his company, the presidency does not include responsibility for community involvement, but the chairmanship does. This man estimated that not only would his activity in community affairs increase but that his influence would also rise. Age is clearly associated with his attainment of this position.

It appears that the nature of the career positions involved tends to make older age a less important factor among the other two elites. Many of the prescribed influentials hold jobs that are subject to new and changing professional standards, and recruitment from the younger population is more frequent. Compulsory retirement systems are also in effect. When these people retire, they are not "kicked upstairs" where they may still have positions of influence. Rather, they are isolated from their former offices and from the concomitant duties and responsibilities in community issues. As for the economic dominants, many of them are branch-plant managers for national concerns. They, too, have compulsory retirement ages, and the positions they hold are sometimes filled by middle-aged or young men who are upwardly mobile in the company, angling for higher jobs in other cities.

Father's occupation. Next to race and sex, one of the most important social determinants of opportunities in life is the circumstances into which a person is born. Father's occupation is a useful index for determining this characteristic. At the national and state levels, the prestige of father's occupation has been shown to be positively related to differential recruitment into political offices.[6] We may hypothesize that, at the community level, father's occupation is equally crucial, if not more so, in determining political status (which includes more than office holding). This importance is due to "community memory," which facilitates the political mobility of the offspring of high-prestige fathers. On the other hand, it may be that low origins can be overcome and that the barriers are not so pronounced in a cosmopolitan, rapidly expanding community like Atlanta.

The distribution of occupational class of fathers among all three elites is distinctly different from the averages of the contemporary period. Although professionals and proprietor-managers in 1900 (nearest census point to average date of birth for the combined elites) formed only 11% of the labor force in the United States, approximately 70% of the attributed and prescribed influentials were born into families where the fathers were so classified. The other 30% had fathers who were, in about equal proportions, skilled laborers, farmers, and clerical-sales workers. Despite the belief that many southern farm boys make good in southern cities, the evidence of their acquiring high political status in Atlanta is slight. In terms of occupational mobility, however, approximately 30% of each of these two elites have advanced, since at present almost all of the status-occupants are in the two higher occupational classifications.

The economic dominants more closely resemble the profile of the "common man." Even among them, however, 35% came from high-prestige homes in terms of fathers' occupations, but the incidence of other, lower prestige backgrounds indicates that *social* mobility at any rate is greatest in this grouping.[7] Having had to overcome early handicaps may be one reason why the economic dominants do not rank high in attributed political status—they are more concerned with economic betterment and the acquisition of economic status superior to that of their fathers. We will explore this thesis in Chapter 9.

Rearing site. The site of a child's rearing helps to determine his social outlook, as well as his life chances. His birthplace in a community may well provide an index to his later integration and reputation in the community. Does the size of the rearing site affect a person's chances of gaining preferred political status? Does the location of his birthplace also influence the possibilities? On neither point can we offer conclusive evidence, but we can show a high relationship between these variables and political status.

Nearly two-thirds of the prescribed influentials and economic dominants and four-fifths of the attributed influentials were reared in towns or cities of more than 25,000 population. There is, furthermore, little indication that rural areas have supplied substantial portions of these elites, despite the fact that three-fifths of the nation's population was rural in 1900. The attributed influentials were least likely to hail from rural areas —only 9% claimed this distinction compared to 17% of the prescribed influentials and 20% of the economic dominants. An urban upbringing, then, is associated with high political status in Atlanta.

Nearly half of the perceived influentials have lived in Atlanta all their lives. If we consider only the top-level attributed influentials, we find that 70% have spent their entire lives in the city, compared with only 17% of the prescribed influentials and 15% of the economic dominants. For the other members of these last two classes, these figures suggest that they or their parents migrated to the Atlanta area in order to advance their fortunes.[8] Natives of Atlanta, therefore, are common only among the attributed influentials.

Education, Occupation, and Income

Although political status is partially conditioned by factors over which people have no control, the basic indices of socio-economic status—education, occupation, and income—do reflect a degree of individual choice and achievement. Obviously the inability of a person's family to help finance his education does limit his educational opportunities, in many cases. But compared to the other variables we have considered, education is a mark of self-achievement, especially higher education levels. And, undoubtedly, education is strongly related to occupation and income. How important are these components for determining membership in the elites of Atlanta?

Education. A high degree of education is a requisite for all three political statuses. A minimum of four-fifths of those in each elite have had at least some collegiate training, and approximately two-fifths have had some graduate or professional training. When compared to the median 10.5 years of education enjoyed by all residents of Atlanta over twenty-five years of age, the high level of education among the elites is even more obvious than at first glance. The incidence of graduate and professional training is probably the most surprising feature of the educational profile. Business executives, however, increasingly are being trained in graduate schools; certainly people in the professions must meet higher and higher requirements to obtain the proper credentials. In general, training beyond the college level is found among those who are utilizing specialized types of knowledge to enhance their political status. Although they have relatively high educational backgrounds, the economic dominants have not had as much formal training as the other two elites. As our analysis of their fathers' occupations suggested, more of the economic dominants tend to be "working their way up."

Where college education was received varies widely among the three groupings. Those who have spent the most time in Georgia, the attributed influentials, are likely to have been educated in Georgia institutions (three-fifths were). Those who go elsewhere are usually the sons of prestige-conscious parents or have been reared in other parts of the country. The decision to attend a local university was an important one for most of the attributed influentials. As Freedgood relates in his discussion of Atlanta's "big mules" (primarily top business influentials):

The choice, says one Atlanta executive, "was basic for us and it's still basic for our sons. You had to decide whether you wanted to go East to the Ivy Leagues and get a better education and maybe a job in New York or stay where you were and build up your contacts and friends. Most of the time, if your family had a business here, or if you planned to go into one, you stayed where you were."[9]

Prescribed influentials had matriculated in nonsouthern schools and Georgia institutions in about equal proportions. Here, place of rearing is a major factor, although there are some southern-raised, professionally trained people who had gone north to school. Finally, those economic dominants who had received higher education had most often matriculated outside Georgia; once again, rearing site was the controlling condition. Just under 20% of the individuals in each elite went to a southern school outside Georgia. In summary, then, an education in Georgia is highly associated with attributed influence, only mildly with prescribed influence, and negatively with economic dominance.

Higher education in Georgia is a rather specialized function conducted mainly at three universities. Two-thirds of those respondents who had had college training in Georgia went either to Georgia Tech or Emory University, both of which are located in Atlanta. If we add to this group those who went to smaller colleges in Atlanta, we find that 80% of the Georgia-educated did not have to leave Atlanta for undergraduate work. The University of Georgia, located less than 100 miles away in Athens, accounts for the third large block, approximately 16%

of the respondents. The other 4% went to two small colleges located elsewhere in the state. This concentration of education in a very few schools breeds gentle "old-school" loyalties and stimulates mild rivalries later on between graduates of different schools. For example, prestigious alumni of Atlanta's colleges who reside in the community often lead financial drives for their respective colleges. Such activities may have repercussions in other areas of community life.

The main point we wish to make here is that a moderate number of attributed and prescribed influentials, especially the former, have emerged from one of three major institutions and in all probability from one in Atlanta itself. These individuals, having received their higher education in the general milieu in which they are to participate as political men, possess an advantage over those who have not shared the common socialization sites and processes.

Economic enterprise. In our thumbnail sketch of Atlanta's economy, we noted its diversification and relative lack of dependence on one or two key industries. This diversification is well reflected in the variety of economic enterprises represented among the attributed influentials (Table 1). Their profile is, in fact, the most evenly distributed of the three elites. We can make no case for the argument that a particular economic specialty dominates the perceived political elite of the community.

Among the prescribed influentials, there is a concentration in the professions and public administration. Most of them are administrative heads of various kinds, who have had specialized training in their fields. There is, of course, a great diversity within this general category. Virtually all the prescribed influentials in commercial enterprises are elective officials or ap-

Table 1. Economic Enterprises of Political Status-Occupants

	Attributed Influentials	Prescribed Influentials	Economic Dominants
Commerce	30%	22%	20%
Manufacturing	15	2	65
Finance	15	2	15
Professional and public administration	34	58	0
Homemaker	0	11	0
Retired	6	4	0
Total	100%	99%	100%
Number	(53)	(46)	(20)

pointees to commissions and boards. With the exception of the commerce category, the profiles of the attributed and prescribed influential incumbents differ substantially.

The outstanding feature of the economic specialization among the economic dominants is the predominance of manufacturing personnel. Two possible reasons for this concentration are apparent. First, although manufacturing is not new to Atlanta, many of the firms represented here are relative late-comers. The gates to political status may not be opened to these new industries immediately. Second, a sizable share of these manufacturing units are branch plants of national corporations. As we shall argue later, "outside" representatives in Atlanta are not so interested in local affairs as are officials of locally owned units. Actually, both of these factors operate to minimize the political status of those economic dominants who are manufacturers.

In breaking down these endeavors, we have listed the primary economic enterprises. This breakdown buries one occupational type whose influence in politics at the state and national levels is well known—the lawyer.

The lawyer is to-day . . . the one indispensable adviser of every responsible policy-maker of our society—whether we speak of the head of a government department or agency, of the executive of a corporation or labor union, of the secretary of a trade or other private association, or even of the humble independent enterpriser or professional man. As such an adviser the lawyer, when informing his policy-maker of what he can or cannot legally do, is in an unassailably strategic position to influence, if not create, policy. . . . For better or worse our decision-makers and our lawyers are bound together in a relation of dependence or of identity.[10]

Whether they are acting in advisory or final decision-making capacities or both, people with legal training are heavily represented in two of the elites. Sixteen (30%) of the perceived elite have had legal training, seven (15%) of the prescribed elite, but none of the economic dominants. Furthermore, the sixteen perceived influentials represent two-thirds of all their group with graduate or professional training. While the incidence of lawyers among those with attributed and prescribed influence is not as great as among elected officers at various governmental levels,[11] it still represents a sizable slice of our elites, especially those who are considered by their peers to have influence. On the surface, at least, the affinity, expertise, special skills, and role indispensability which give lawyers differential advantages in other geographical areas and at other levels of policy-making are also operative in Atlanta.

If the three status-groups show a marked distribution in economic endeavor, they reveal an even greater one in income. While 58% of the prescribed influentials reported annual incomes less than $20,000, only 17% of the attributed influentials and 11% of the economic dominants were in that bracket. At the other extreme, 60% of the perceived elite and 42% of the economic dominants reported incomes over $50,000 compared with only 16% of the prescribed influentials.[12]

Although the median income even of the prescribed influentials by far surpasses the median for the Atlanta area, income is not so instrumental for achieving prescribed as for achieving attributed influence. The definition of his office gives the former a presumptive right to a politically influential role, regardless of his income. For the latter group, however, people who for the most part follow other occupations, sizable incomes seem necessary for two reasons. First, prestige accompanies high income, if legitimately earned, and prestige is a basic ingredient of status. Second, unless a man's occupation relates directly to participation in community decision-making (as is quite often the case with lawyers), a certain minimum income is necessary to liberate his time for participation in community affairs. Both prestige and the opportunity to participate at a high level are thus derivatives of high income for the attributed elite.

That high income is not the sole determinant of perceived influence, however, is demonstrated by the economic dominants. Two-fifths of them earn more than $50,000, and approximately nine-tenths earn more than $20,000. Yet they neither hold important public or quasi-public positions nor are they commonly perceived as being very influential. While high income itself, then, is a concomitant of attributed influence, it is by no means a single causal factor; that is, reputed influence is associated with high income, but high income is not necessarily associated with reputed influence.

These three indices—education, occupation, and income—are objective measures of social class or socio-economic status. The subjects were also asked to designate their own social-class statuses on a five-point scale, ranging from upper class through lower class.

Not unexpectedly, a few refused to classify themselves. In most instances, they exhibited obvious signs of upper-class distinction, but they were reticent about admitting class-consciousness. For those who did classify themselves, the distribution is, as might be expected, heavily weighted toward the upper end of the scale. No one ranked himself as lower or lower middle class. Respondents who ranked themselves as middle class come from the relatively lower-income group of prescribed influentials. Despite the social taboo of admitting to upper class status, nearly one-half of the economic dominants and slightly over one-third of those with attributed influence confessed to this distinction. While we make no assumptions about the behavioral consequences of these class ratings, we can point out that the vast majority of our actors consider themselves to be of higher social status than the "average" person in the community. Additionally, if self-designation be accepted as a reliable guide, the relationship between social status and perceived political status is not invariable. That is, the group that designated themselves the highest socially—the economic dominants—are not widely acknowledged to be men of power.

Other Social Characteristics

We next consider some variables over which the individual has even more control. This section deals with length of residence, partisanship, religious preference, and mass-media consumption.

Length of residence. The elites differ in how long they have lived in Atlanta. Eighty-five percent of the perceived influentials have lived there more than twenty years, compared to 65% of the prescribed influentials and only 45% of the economic dominants. Normally, the longer a person lives in an area, the more opportunity the community has to observe him, and the more frequent are his chances to show his mettle. Respect and deference are also accorded to "old timers." It is not surprising, therefore, that virtually all the perceived influentials have lived the major portions of their adult lives in the Atlanta area. Although Atlanta has boomed economically for the past twenty years, thus creating an influx of high-level professional and business people, the newcomers have not necessarily been granted high political status. Highlighting this point are the comparatively short lengths of residence for the economic dominants, who have the least apparent political influence among the actors under study. The "old timers" have kept enough major Atlanta institutions under control so that they still can claim higher status.[13]

This point is an important one. Many of those who hold important economic posts in Atlanta are "outsiders." As Freedgood remarks:

They are the chief regional representatives of big national corporations or, as they sometimes call themselves, the "corporate nomads"— men who have been sent to Atlanta to establish branch plants, offices, and warehouses. These managers have descended on Atlanta for something like the reason that Sherman did: strategic location.

The typical nomad is (as Atlantans might put it) "scatterbred": he may have come from anywhere but probably grew up in the North, Midwest, or West and, in any case, usually views Atlanta as simply another of the many "waiting towns" he must traverse in his climb upward to company headquarters in New York, Chicago, or Detroit.[14]

Freedgood further points out that the corporate nomad simply carries out the orders of distant superiors, while the locally based economic titan has considerable economic power in his own right. Of the economic dominants included in our study, the 55% who have lived in Atlanta less than twenty years (most of them less than ten years) fit this pattern, except that they are almost exclusively in the manufacturing field.

Partisanship. Although political party preference is not, strictly speaking, a socio-economic characteristic, we include the topic here because of its high correlation with socio-economic status and because it helps to complete the over-all social profile of our elites. The emerging Republicanism of the South in recent presidential elections has been largely a product of the urban vote.[15] Because of the strong traditions of state politics, however, only small inroads have been made on Democratic domination of state elections. We would expect to find in our Atlanta respondents clear evidence of this nascent Republicanism because of the cosmopolitanism, the highly urban nature of the community, and the high socio-economic standing of the status-occupants.

The data support this hypothesis. We have broken down

the three elites into the basic categories (see pp. 24-5) because there are important differences in this case. At the state level, from 75% to 88% of the first- and second-level perceived influentials and government officials identify with the Democratic party, while only 45% of the economic dominants and 50% of the civic staffers do. Now it is true that this difference may merely mean that the last two groups consider themselves independent of a particular faction that dominates the Democratic party. A more likely explanation is that they are so estranged from the Democratic party itself that they do not identify with it even in one-party Georgia.

Turning to the national level, civic-staff personnel and economic dominants intensify their proclivities for the Republican and independent designations, as do all the other groupings. Indeed, 70% of the first-level attributed influentials claim to be national Republicans. The government officials, whose livelihood tends to be more closely connected with party politics and who are also the least cosmopolitan, show only a slight drop in Democratic identification from state (79%) to national level (67%). If we assume for a moment that all five status-groups represent some sort of community leadership and that being an independent is in reality a sign of potential or real Republicanism (Eisenhower Democrats for example), then the evidence of a latent pool of Republican leadership in national elections is very clear in Atlanta.

A sizable number in each grouping indicated that their friends were either Republicans or independents at the national level. In fact, a modest majority of the first-level attributed influentials and economic dominants made this statement. Coupled with our information about party preference, this answer suggests the presence of a community (in terms of process) of Republicanism in Atlanta, of which a good portion of our subjects are a part. Most of them are not conspicuous in their Republicanism, however, so that the consequences of their identification have, until recently, been minimal for the politics of the community itself. One perceived influential was a state official in the Republican party. His position and activities associated with the party were not taken too seriously by his peers at the time. Nevertheless, the "silk-stocking district," which sent a Republican senator to the Georgia state legislature in 1963, is the home of many of the more affluent people under study.

Religious features. Another social trait that shows differential representation among the elites is religious affiliation. From what we have demonstrated so far about the social and economic characteristics of the three classes of actors, we would expect that in religious preferences they would continue to fall into three fairly distinct patterns. Almost everyone interviewed has a religious preference, and Protestantism dominates. Among Protestants, though, the high-prestige Episcopal and Presbyterian denominations are preferred by well over one-half of the attributed influentials. Nearly all the prescribed influentials are Protestants, but they distribute their preferences throughout the spectrum of denominations. Those economic dominants who are Protestants (55%) also spread their choices.

Eight of the fifty-three attributed influentials are Catholics or Jews, an indication of the cosmopolitan character of Atlanta, compared with some other southern cities.[16] The percentage of Jews and Catholics is proportionally representative of the community at large, since the two groups together compose about 15% of the city's population. Deviation in religious preference from the strong norms of the South does not prevent attainment of preferred political status in Atlanta. These eight individuals, however, have excelled in special ways. Three were associated with Rich's, a retail firm pre-eminent in the entire South; one paid the highest *ad valorem* taxes in the city; two were members of a law firm with perhaps the highest prestige in the community —Spalding, Sibley, Troutman, Meadow and Smith; another was an executive of the Coca-Cola Company, which occupies a unique position of prestige in the community; and another was the major representative of organized labor. Thus they have not only had to succeed, but to exceed the success of others in their respective endeavors. Even if they have had to excel in striking ways, these representatives from minority religions *have* gained recognition, and the top of the perceived power structure appears to be more representative of the total population than is normal in the South.

As with other characteristics, the religious pattern of the economic dominants again bears more resemblance to those of regions outside the South than to that of Atlanta. Forty per cent of them have a Jewish or Catholic preference. There are no data to support the thesis that these preferences help to bar these people from attaining the status of attributed influence. Rather, the heavy incidence of branch managers and relative newcomers among the economic dominants is a more plausible explanation,, (discussed in more detail below).

    Reading habits. The type of leisure-time reading a person engages in tends to affect his outlook on public affairs, not only at the international, national, and state levels, but also at the local level. Whether the resulting influence is mere reinforcement of previous opinions or stimulus to new thought, exposure to printed media deserves consideration. Almost all the respondents reported reading both the *Atlanta Constitution* and the *Atlanta Journal,* which are jointly owned but occasionally take different editorial stands on public issues. The interviewees also reported on the out-of-state papers they read. As Table 2 indicates, the respondents are quite cosmopolitan in their reading tastes.

    Differences are apparent, however. Those with prescribed influence are the least sophisticated in terms of newspaper reading. Many of them confine their horizons to Atlanta, and they

Table 2. Cosmopolitanism as Measured by Reading Habits of Political Status-Occupants

	ATTRIBUTED INFLUENTIALS		PRESCRIBED INFLUENTIALS		ECONOMIC DOMINANTS
	First Level	Second Level	Government Officials	Civic Staff	
Outside Newspapers					
Wall Street Journal	30%	27%	25%	18%	40%
Prestige newspaper*	15	30	29	36	10
Wall Street Journal and prestige newspaper	50	15	0	18	25
None	5	28	46	28	25
Total	100%	100%	100%	100%	100%
Number	(20)	(33)	(24)	(22)	(20)
Magazines					
Light only	0%	0%	38%	14%	21%
News and light	50	55	41	41	58
Class** and news or light	50	45	21	45	21
Total	100%	100%	100%	100%	100%
Number	(20)	(31)	(24)	(22)	(19)

    *Includes New York Times, New York Herald Tribune, Washington Post, and The Christian Science Monitor.
    **Includes such magazines as Harper's, The Atlantic, The Reporter, National Geographic Magazine, Saturday Review, The New Republic, Holiday, and so forth.*

do not have the broader interests of the other two elites. On the other hand, many of the others have business interests that especially dictate their reading of the *Wall Street Journal,* and they are thus exposed to a much different set of stimuli from that of the prescribed influentials.

As for magazine reading, everyone appears to read at least one magazine regularly. We divided the respondents into those who read only light *(Life, The Saturday Evening Post, Sports Illustrated, House & Home,* and so forth) or news magazines *(Time, Newsweek, U. S. News and World Report)* and those who read one or both of these types plus at least one "class" magazine *(Harpers Magazine, The Atlantic, The Reporter, National Geographic Magazine, Saturday Review, The New Republic, Holiday,* and so forth). Those with attributed influence clearly emerge as the most cosmopolitan in their reading, with almost half of them including "class" magazines in their reading. In view of the more extra-community-oriented profile of the economic dominants, we might have expected them to be higher in their "class" reading. Again, however, their preoccupation with the business, especially corporate, world of which they are a part seems to limit their horizons. They read the *Wall Street Journal* and the news and light magazines to keep up with developments in the business world and the public world in general. They do not, like many of the attributed influentials, exhibit sophisticated tastes in the social, political, and cultural worlds.

Robert Merton, in his Rovere study, divided influentials in interpersonal relations partly on the basis of their reading habits. It was the reading of a news magazine like *Time* and of the class magazines that distinguished the cosmopolitans from the locals. Light magazines like *Life* and *Reader's Digest* appeared with equal frequency among his two categories.[17] If we apply this standard in Atlanta, the local government officials, who have by far the highest incidence of purely light reading, most resemble Merton's locals. Recalling that government officials also read fewer out-of-state newspapers, this preference heightens the picture of them as less cosmopolitan than the other groups. Add their stronger attachment to the Democratic party, and we perceive that government officials are the most locally oriented individuals in our study.

Overlap of Economic and Political Status

Some power-structure studies have examined the overlap or correlation in the community between high political status and (by inference or demonstration) political influence on the one hand, and top economic status on the other.[18] This correlation provides an implicit test of the thesis that economic position determines political status and political power. Our research procedures enable us to test this notion for Atlanta. As reported, forty-one people were designated as economic dominants in the Atlanta metropolitan area. None of them has the status of a prescribed influential as we have defined the term. Some of them were among the attributed elite, however. By examining the association of economic dominance with attributed political influence, we have a measure of the congruence between high economic position and high political status. Since data could be obtained from other sources, a few individuals who were not interviewed are included in this analysis. To facilitate the analysis, we will anticipate at some points the behavioral data to be presented in later chapters.

Thirty-seven per cent of the forty-one economic dominants are also attributed influentials. On this basis, the probability of any given top economic position being associated with high reputed influence is moderate, about one in three. That is not to say that many of those with attributed influence do not hold fairly important economic positions. It does demonstrate, however, that possession of a major economic position does not automatically entitle one to high political status based on attributed influence. Viewing the proportions from another angle strengthens the point. Of the fifty-seven operationally defined attributed influentials, only 21% hold positions of economic dominance. If gaining a reputation for influence were only a matter of occupying a major economic post, the fifty-seven attributed influentials should consist mainly of economic titans.

Why do some economic dominants gain preferred political status while others do not? Basically, we are asking why there are what Lipset and Bendix call "status discrepancies."[19] These discrepancies occur when people do not occupy comparable positions in various status systems. In the case at hand, the question is why some individuals who are ranked high in the

economic status hierarchy are not similarly ranked in the political status hierarchy (bearing in mind that different operations
were used to arrive at the respective rankings). One of the most
discriminating answers rests in the organization of the firms in
which the economic elite operate. Economic notables in Atlanta
who possess the status of attributed influentials are most often
associated with locally oriented firms which have their home
offices in the city. In most instances, these firms were founded
in Atlanta, their leading officials are long-time residents of the
area, and the enterprises enjoy high prestige in the community.

On the other hand, those economic dominants who are not
perceived influentials may or may not be associated with local
firms on an almost equal ratio. Visibility and prestige of firm
may explain part of the variance. A more likely interpretation
relates the general aspects of firm characteristics and community
participation to political status. All those economic dominants
not associated with local firms are branch managers for national
corporations—"corporate nomads." In Atlanta, there is not a
strong tradition of these managers becoming actively involved
in community policy-making. One reason is that high-status
people have been somewhat loath to accept these people into
the upper reaches of decision-making, partly because the fortunes of national corporations are not so inextricably linked
with the development of the city as are local firms. As will become apparent in later chapters, a perception of influence rests
in part on actual participation and influence in community
issues. If the corporate nomads are denied entry into the upper
echelons of structure of power, it is unlikely that they will be
perceived as power wielders.

There are, of course, exceptions to the practice of shutting
out the outsiders. If a person comes in with a particularly high
office in his company, he may be accorded high status and more
ready access to power. The more economically strategic the firm,
the more likely that will be the case. One perceived influential,
for example, came to Atlanta a few years ago as a vice-president
of the Lockheed Corporation and manager of the local plant,
the largest single employer in the metropolitan area. Although
he had no intense desire to participate in local affairs, he slowly
became involved in projects ranging from the mayoralty campaign to urban renewal and educational drives.

A second complex of reasons why branch managers do not

attain high status lies in a corporate aversion to participation. Writing of efforts to handle the problems of mushrooming urbanism, William H. Whyte notes that

on one point, however, there is widespread agreement. Executives of national corporations—except where the corporation's home office is in the city—have not been much help. Big corporations have been making a great point of community participation—some have put vice presidents in charge of such activities—but big corporation executives are more loath than anyone to mess in anything that smacks of politics, and their community-relations effort is apt to be on the innocuous level of open-house days at the plant, children's tours, and free use of the company's baseball diamond.[20]

Actually the two causes reinforce each other. If the "corporate nomad" gives no indication that he will become active, then he will probably be excluded from major policy-making. By the same token, if he comes in with expectations of participating and is then rebuffed, he may well cease his attempts at participation. An example occurred in Atlanta when representatives of the semi-official Traffic and Safety Commission sought to involve the managers of major automotive assembly plants in a safety program. Apparently taking their own cues from their home offices, the plant managers refused the overture. These managers were not often considered for subsequent policy-making committees or posts in other substantive areas. Branch managers, then, tend not to be active both because of certain obstacles in the community to effective participation and because of corporate reticence. Such inactivity serves to prevent inclusion in the reputed elite.

Another tangible factor, though, is the physical location of the primary office or work-center of the firm. The firms were divided into those with offices in the area commonly known as the central business district (CBD) and those with major work centers away from the downtown area. Only three of the twenty people working outside the CBD, compared with twelve of the twenty-one within the CBD, were among the attributed elite (Table 3). Although being in the CBD is not, therefore, a guarantee that the economic dominant will be a perceived influential, it is almost essential to gain the designation.

We need not look far to explain this finding. The downtown area is the heart of Atlanta's financial and commercial institutions. While there is no assurance that such enterprises will be more involved than, for example, manufacturing plants located on the outskirts of town, such is traditionally the case.

Table 3. Relationship between Perceived Influence and Characteristics of the Firms of All Economic Dominants

Characteristics of the Firms	Perceived Influentials	Not Perceived Influentials	Total	Number
Firm Headquarters				
Local	52%	48	100%	(23)
Regional or National	17%	83	100%	(18)
Main Work Center				
CBD	57%	43	100%	(21)
Non-CBD	15%	85	100%	(20)
Type of Product				
Nonmanufacturing	55%	45	100%	(22)
Manufacturing	16%	84	100%	(19)

Financial and commercial establishments deal with literally thousands of people daily, their activities are intimately involved with those of countless other economic enterprises, and their success rests primarily upon a locus of product consumption *inside* rather than outside the community.

Another conditioning factor is propinquity. The downtown businessman has convenient personal access to civic and governmental representatives, while the person who works on the fringes of town must take a long drive downtown for such contacts. Finally, it is no secret that many of Atlanta's problems lie in economic threats to the CBD from the shopping centers and from traffic congestion and urban blight near the downtown core. An almost irresistible tendency to focus on the CBD's problems demands at least some involvement by leading economic dominants of the CBD.

We have suggested that the type of economic endeavor might be associated with the differential status ratings. For those engaging in nonmanufacturing enterprises, the probability of high status is about even (Table 3), but for those in manufacturing the likelihood is small that they will achieve high status. Those engaged in manufacturing are, with one exception, those whose work lies outside the CBD, so that much of the discussion regarding location also applies here. Dependence on product consumption outside the community appears to be a particularly strong force in lessening extensive participation.

Actually, the three factors—organization of the firm, physical location, and type of product—are closely interrelated variables that work to reinforce one another in determining an economic dominant's political status in the community. Of the three, type of product is perhaps the most important. Certain firms that are ordinarily located in the CBD—banks, commercial and retail outlets, real-estate and contracting operations, and communications concerns—are almost inevitably more visible politically and are drawn into more areas of community policymaking than are some of the heavy manufacturing plants that tend to locate outside the CBD. And in Atlanta, the large establishments in the CBD also tend to be "home-owned," a condition that may not exist in many other urban centers.

But what of the economic dominants who are with locally owned firms, located in the CBD, and engaged in nonmanufacturing enterprises, but are nevertheless not perceived as influentials? Personal predilections undoubtedly come into play here. One of the questions in a personality inventory left with the respondents at the conclusion of the formal interview asked them to indicate their interest in politics on a four-point scale ranging from "very much interested" down to "not at all interested." Two-thirds or more of the prescribed and attributed influentials selected the highest category of interest. In dramatic contrast, only 12% of the economic dominants chose that category, with characteristics of their firms accounting for little difference in the responses. The low saliency of political matters for these economic dominants therefore seems to inhibit their involvement in community issues and thus weakens their prospects of being included in the ranks of the attributed influentials by virtue of participation. Even if the economic notable is in the "right" kind of enterprise, his apolitical nature may keep him out of community decision-making.

A brief conclusion about the relationships between social features and political status can be drawn from the data presented in this chapter. In general, the attributed influentials have the most privileged backgrounds, the deepest roots in the community, and the highest socio-economic status. The economic dominants are next to the attributed influentials in socioeconomic status, but they have the weakest ties to the community and the least privileged backgrounds of all three status-groups. Occupying an intermediate position, the prescribed influentials do not have so high a socio-economic status as the other two elites, but their ties to the community are stronger, and their social backgrounds somewhat more privileged than those of the economic notables. A large majority of the actors in each elite have far above-average social backgrounds and socio-economic status. While the attributed influentials tend to have the most cosmopolitan interests of all the actors, the economic dominants deviate the most from some typical southern patterns of life. The prescribed influentials, particularly the government officials, tend to be the most provincial. Different over-all social patterns are thus connected with the backgrounds and contemporary characteristics of the three major elites. To this extent, some parts of the patterns may be termed requisites or determinants of political status, in addition to those that simply describe politically relevant social aspects of the elites.

Finally, there is a high relationship between membership in the economic elite and being an attributed influential for those in home-owned firms located in the CBD and tending to be of nonmanufacturing types. The incidence of congruence between the upper ranges in the economic and political status systems in only moderate, however. Status divergencies are more the rule than the exception.

NOTES

1. Donald R. Matthews, *The Social Background of Decision-Makers*, "Doubleday Short Studies in Political Science" (Garden City: Doubleday & Company, Inc., 1954), pp. 20-55.

2. The dynamic aspects of such relations have also been noted on occasion. Robert Daland charts the changing social composition of a city commission in a rapidly growing southern community in *Dixie City: A Portrait of Political Leadership* (University: Bureau of Public Administration, University of Alabama, 1956), pp. 5-17. For a study showing the consequences to social status of being a city councilman, see Gilbert Brown, "The Relationship of Elective Political Office in the City of Redlands, California, to the Status Concept" (Unpublished Ph.D. thesis, University of Southern California, 1956).

3. A prime reason why the converse is not true is that it is frequently the *combination* of various social characteristics (along with factors of personality, the political environment, chance, and so forth) that leads to attainment of a certain status; one attribute alone seldom assures such achievement.

4. Christopher Sower, *et al.*, *Community Involvement* (New York: The Free Press of Glencoe, 1957), pp. 235-6.

5. She has subsequently retired.

6. Matthews, *op. cit.*, pp. 23-4.

7. See Seymour Martin Lipset and Reinhard Bendix, *Social Mobility in Industrial Society* (Berkeley and Los Angeles: University of California Press, 1959), chap. 4, for data on the social mobility of the American business elite.

8. Further analyses indicated that the immigrants to Atlanta came from urban centers smaller than Atlanta. This indication appears to confirm the Lipset and Bendix suggestion that the large metropolis attracts, among others, a minority of well-educated migrants from smaller-sized areas who can compete with the natives for high status vocational positions, especially in the professions. *Ibid.*, chap. 8.

9. Seymour Freedgood, "Life in Buckhead," *Fortune* (September, 1961), p. 188.

10. Harold D. Lasswell and M. S. McDougal, "Legal Education and Public Policy," in Lasswell, ed., *The Analysis of Political Behavior* (London: Routledge, Kegan Paul Ltd., 1948), p. 27, quoted in Matthews, *op. cit.*, p. 31.

11. Joseph A. Schlesinger, "Lawyers and American Politics: A Clarified View," *Midwest Journal of Political Science*, I (May, 1957), 26-39.

12. For those readers particularly interested in income distribution, we offer the following figures: 45% of the top-level attributed influentials had incomes over $100,000; 6% of those at the secondary level; 15% of the economic dominants; and none in the other groups.

13. Floyd Hunter notes this tendency in many southern communities in his "Community Organization: Lever for Institutional Change?" in Rupert B. Vance and Nicholas J. Demereth, eds., *The Urban South* (Chapel Hill: University of North Carolina Press, 1954), p. 262.

14. Freedgood, *op. cit.*, p. 110.

15. See Louis Harris, *Is There a Republican Majority?* (New York: Harper & Row, Publishers, 1954), chap. 5; Donald S. Strong, *Urban Republicanism in the South* (University: Bureau of Public Administration, University of Alabama, 1960); and Bernard Cosman, "Presidential Republicanism in the South," *Journal of Politics*, XXIV (May, 1962), 303-22.

16. Raleigh, North Carolina, for example, had a comparable figure of only 1%, according to research carried out by the author in 1959.

17. Robert K. Merton, *Social Theory and Social Structure* (rev. and enlarged ed.; New York: The Free Press of Glencoe, 1957), pp. 406-8.

18. Notably Robert O. Schulze and Leonard U. Blumberg, "The Determination of Local Power Elites," *American Journal of Sociology*, 63 (November 1959), 290-6; Robert A. Dahl, *Who Governs?* (New Haven: Yale University Press, 1961), pp. 63-84; A. H. Birch, *Small Town Politics* (London: Oxford University Press, 1959), pp. 34-40; and, of course, Floyd Hunter, *Community Power Structure* (Chapel Hill: University of North Carolina Press, 1953), especially pp. 26-113.

19. Lipset and Bendix, *op. cit.*, pp. 64-8, 275-7.

20. William H. Whyte, "Introduction," in Editors of Fortune, *The Exploding Metropolis* (Garden City: Doubleday & Company, Inc., 1958), pp. xviii-xix.

4

POLITICIZATION

AND

POLITICAL STATUS

THE PRECEDING CHAPTER described some pertinent aspects of characteristics and social backgrounds of the three major elites. This chapter focuses on such other correlates of political status as governmental position, activity in politicized organizations, participation in community issues, and politically oriented interpersonal communication. To determine the extent and nature of the politicized behavior of the different groups is the object. Here we begin to explore the role-behavior accompanying certain statuses.

We begin by making two assumptions to facilitate analysis. We assume initially that occupancy of a government post automatically gives the occupant certain resources with which to participate in policy-making. Second, we postulate that participation in politicized organizations, communication channels, and substantive issues is a manifestation of political power orientation and that, roughly speaking, a higher degree of participation signifies more power-oriented behavior (politicization). Notice that we do not claim that positive power increases with participation; it may or may not. Rather, participation is viewed as an index of power orientation. As an act of power has been defined—a successful attempt to exert influence on outcomes—participation is a *sine qua non* of power, although not necessarily of the more encompassing term "influence."

Overlap of Attributed Influence and Ranking Government Position

Examining the overlap between high political status and occupancy of formal governmental positions has been another preoccupation of power-structure inquiries. In reputational studies, this interest stems in part from an attempt to determine if the governmental office holders are exercising primary or secondary power. That is, to what extent do government personnel exercise self-generated influence over outcomes rather than responding to others in the power structure who are utilizing government officials to achieve their own ends? Usually the conclusion has been that, if government officials are not among the reputed elite, then they wield only secondary power.

Our rationale for examining the degree of overlap has dual significance. First, as with the economic dominants, there is the question of whether there are status congruencies at this point. To what extent are people at the apex of the governmental institutions also at the top of the perceived structure of power? Among what kinds of office holders does such integration occur? Second, holding a governmental position is a mark of high politicization. The extent of office holding by attributed influentials provides, therefore, one significant measure of their politicization.

The final list of major government officials for Atlanta and Fulton County contained the names of forty individuals, one less than the total of economic dominants. Fifteen of the forty (38%) are also attributed influentials. The proportion of congruence is almost identical with that between economic dominants and attributed influentials. Again, a key institutional position—in this case a governmental post—does not automatically entitle its incumbent to a high attributed status. Once more there is evidence of status discrepancy at the upper reaches of two structures.

Approaching this problem from another perspective substantiates the point. The fifteen government officials constitute only 26% of all the fifty-seven attributed influentials. There is thus an unwillingness to concede that perceived influence derives only from holding a major governmental post. As there was no one-to-one correlation between top economic position and high attributed political status, so there is no such relationship between a leading government position and membership in the reputed elite. At the same time, the amount of overlap is enormously greater than would occur by chance in a metropolis of this size. Holding a governmental position is, therefore, moderately related to reputed influence. Taken together, incumbents of major positions in the sectors of government and economic enterprise constitute slightly over half (53%) of all the attributed influentials.

Certain kinds of government official are more likely than others to be vested with high attributed influence. Table 4

Table 4. Relationship between Features of Major Government Positions and Attributed or Prescribed Influence

Feature of Position	Attributed Influence	Prescribed Influence	Total	Number
Professional	14%	86	100%	(14)
Nonprofessional	50%	50	100%	(26)
Appointive	27%	73	100%	(26)
Elective	57%	43	100%	(14)
City Office	27%	73	100%	(22)
Extra-city office	50%	50	100%	(18)

demonstrates that those who hold full-time professional positions tend not to be attributed high influence. The two professionals who do have such influence are the ranking administrators of the Atlanta and Fulton County school systems. Professionals traditionally command deference in the educational field. As for the nonprofessionals, they have an even chance of remaining either in the prescribed or the attributed class. For the most part, the nonprofessionals with perceived influence are chairmen of lay boards or ranking elective officials; the balance of the nonprofessionals are chairmen of lower prestige boards or hold minor elective posts.

Elective officials as a whole are more often found in the attributive than in the purely prescriptive elite (Table 4). They include the mayor, two county commissioners, two members of the state legislative delegation, two chairmen of strategic aldermanic committees, and the chairman of the city school board. There is thus a widespread distribution by geographical governmental units, even though the city itself supplies the majority of the votes in all elections in which these men compete. The other elective officials include four aldermen, the elections board chairman, and a state legislator.

The appointive officials considered to have high influence include the two educational professionals and five chairmen of ranking lay boards in the community. The remaining appointees include thirteen full-time professional governmental employees and six chairmen of relatively less important lay boards.

It is necessary to make one final distinction between government officials serving the city of Atlanta exclusively and those who serve Fulton County or both county and city and, in one case, three counties (Table 4). Those responsible to extra-city jurisdictions are found in equal ratio among the attributed and prescribed influentials, while those serving the city alone are found predominantly in the prescribed elite. In absolute terms, there is a tendency to select as attributed influentials those individuals who serve the larger geopolitical units; nine of the fifteen officials among the attributed influentials hail from extra-city jurisdictions. As Atlanta's problems expand outward and as more comprehensive governing bodies are established, even more deference may be expected toward extra-city officials.

Why should the nonprofessional, elective, and extra-city officials be placed more often in the perceived elite than are their fellow officials? The answer rests primarily in job status. Professionals are mainly public administrators. They are considered by others and by themselves to be employees of local government. One professional, when asked how he viewed his relationship to the "acknowledged" men of power in the community, summed it up in this fashion: "I consider myself a hired hand. I could grab the ball and run with it. But sooner or later they would catch up with me."

This particular professional is neither self-effacing nor cowardly. Yet to him and his colleagues the status gap between them and the nonprofessionals is apparent. Nonprofessionals are either elective office-holders or appointees to lay boards. They are not "hired hands" in the scheme of governmental organizations. Only where administrative roles are prominent or of wide-ranging importance, as with school administrators, are the professionals' reputations for influence likely to be widespread.[1]

Elective officials hold an edge over appointees for partly the same reasons. They often have a hand in the appointing and dismissing of professional appointees, a fact that gives them *a priori* superior ranks within their organizations. Then, too, they have a base of support and influence in a readily visible constituency. Although they may not have met a payroll, they have met the test of the polls, and they are highly visible so that their public actions can be monitored by many parties. Finally, they are frequently the authorized decision-makers on a wide range of issues. They are "supposed" to be influential.

The reason extra-city officials are regarded as more influential than those strictly within the city arises partly from the prominence accorded elective officials outside the city. It proceeds also from the fact that some of the most powerful quasi-independent boards encompass more than one unit of government each. Most include more than the city of Atlanta. Within the political city itself, only the mayor, the chairman of the board of education, and perhaps two or three ranking aldermen, have bases of influence deemed sufficient for recognition as influentials. But beyond the city government, there are a number of elective and highly strategic lay committee chairmanships that attract recognition and serve as springboards for acts of power.

To present a comprehensive picture of overlapping membership between the legal government and the broader perceived influence structure of Atlanta we must note that a number of other actors also overlap the two structures. Several of the perceived elite serve on the lay committees whose chairmen occupy strategic positions. Adding all those on the committees who are also attributed influentials (fourteen in all) to the overlapping membership list leads to a total of twenty-nine (51%) of the fifty-seven attributed influentials serving in local government either in elective or appointive capacities.

Furthermore, ten other perceived influentials had held

governmental positions in the past, making a total of thirty-nine of the total fifty-seven, or 68%, who are or have been government officials in some capacity in the Atlanta area. The relative ranking of those with attributed influence—top level or second level—makes little difference in the probability of their having had governmental experience. Of the twenty-three at the first level, seventeen (74%) have held or presently hold governmental positions, while at the second level, twenty-two of the thirty-four (65%) have had such experience. This evidence strongly suggests that the perceived influentials of Atlanta, rather than being withdrawn from operations of the formal government and working behind the scenes, actually become involved both in professional and lay capacities in the formal governmental structure. They are highly politicized in this respect.[2]

Participation in Politicized Organizations

Robert Lane suggests three senses in which joining a local association is a political act:

(1) It supports the pluralistic bases of political power and group representation. (2) It opens up a two-way channel of political communication between memberships and elites. (3) It is a means of expressing personal political interests.[3]

He also classifies such organizations into three types—the political club, the quasi-political organization that takes stands on public issues, and other types that serve to stimulate politically oriented discussion. Atlanta has no strong political clubs as such. The influence of the "49" and "101" clubs to which Hunter refers[4] has diminished thanks to the rearrangement of political boundaries in the area. Another organization, the "Cactus Club," is of post-World War II vintage and is led by lawyers. Its primary task is to adopt a list of preferred candidates in local elections and then to circulate the list to interested parties. Estimates on the vote-drawing ability of the list range from 250 to 1500. The influential Atlanta Negro Voters League is perhaps the most important political "club."

Civic organizations of the good government-civic, the business-civic, and the welfare types clearly fall within the quasi-political classification. Atlanta's plethora of quasi-political organizations offers ample illustration of why participation in them is a political act. The following example depicts a typical means by which quasi-political associations of the business-civic type seek to affect policy outcomes. This particular event represents an exercise of veto power.

One of the problems most of the downtown organizations are concerned with is on-street and off-street parking. Shortly before the time of this study, the Atlanta Traffic and Transportation Commission, which has legal status, adopted a proposal on off-street parking contrary to the aims of at least one of the downtown organizations. A city alderman sent a copy of the resolution to the executive secretary of the organization. He, in turn, had an executive board meeting called, at which time he presented the case and expressed his point of view. After the board went on record opposing the resolution, the executive secretary and the principal officers made contact with three other downtown organizations with whom an agreement was worked out for a common stand on the proposal. These organizations requested and received a public hearing before the appropriate aldermanic committee. The executive secretary and three officers of the first organization, as well as representatives of the other associations appeared at the hearing. Their protestations defeated the proposal.[5]

We are interested in the differential rates of participation in local associations among the elites. It seems fair to say that the higher the rate of participation the higher the politicization of the individual in the civic organizational field. Table 5 gives data on different measures of such participation. Because the breakdowns are extremely revealing, top-level influentials are separated from those at the second level, and government officials from civic-staff personnel.

When compared with average rates of participation in America, the frequencies for all the groups are high.[6] Intergroup differences in this type of politicization do exist, however. For example, some striking dissimilarities emerge for memberships in civic organizations. Contrary to what might be expected, the first-level attributed influentials actually hold more memberships than those at the second level. Particularly striking is the low incidence of organization memberships among government officials. Apparently, they do not need such memberships to supply a base of strength in the same way that the attributed influentials do. Additionally, their predominant status as paid professionals of local government tends to bar them from primarily business-oriented organizations. Civic-staff personnel, while not so active as attributed influentials, are still consider-

Table 5. Rates of Participation in Local Associations

	ATTRIBUTED INFLUENTIALS		PRESCRIBED INFLUENTIALS		ECONOMIC DOMINANTS
	First Level	Second Level	Government Officials	Civic Staff	
Civic organization memberships					
0-2	15%*	36%	83%	41%	50%
3 or more	85	64	17	59	50
Offices and committee memberships					
0	15%	30%	56%	23%	25%
1-3	45	36	31	50	55
4 or more	40	33	13	27	20
Past offices					
0	20%	15%	39%	27%	30%
1-2	35	45	30	41	35
3 or more	45	39	30	31	35
Social club memberships					
0	5%	12%	56%	50%	5%
1-2	40	48	35	41	55
3 or more	55	39	9	9	40
State and national association memberships					
0	15%	12%	0%	4%	45%
1-4	60	48	61	91	55
5 or more	25	39	39	4	0
Number	(20)	(33)	(23)	(22)	(20)

*Percentages for each group total 100% (or 99%) under each subheading.

ably more active than government officials and somewhat more active than the economic dominants, who fall between the extremes of many and few memberships. Notable also is the fact that the group with the highest objective social status, the attributed influentials, holds the largest number of memberships.

One might argue that membership itself is not a necessary sign of overt participation in an organization. Holding offices and serving on committees do constitute better indices of participation, although membership itself can be parlayed into differential access to various types of influentials. Actually, a distribution similar to that for membership is found for offices and committee positions (Table 5). The first-level attributed influentials still rank highest and the government officials lowest. Although the economic dominants score relatively well on this index, we shall see later that this area is the only one in which they do participate on a nearly equal basis with the other elites.

Distribution of those who have held offices in the past follows the profile already outlined, with the exception that government officials in this instance rank closer to other status-holders. The explanation for this greater congruency lies in the tendency for government officials, upon taking office, to dissociate themselves from the civic organizations of which they have formerly been members. This tendency is particularly strong among elective officials and much less so among appointive ones. Elective officials may have used the civic associations for gaining office. Once their offices are secured, they perhaps do not think it proper to maintain membership or hold office in such associations, or they no longer see the need for it in terms of furthering their own interests.

With the exception of civic-staff personnel, participation is low in neighborhood or suburban organizations (not shown). Civic staffers score well in this respect, primarily because there are several women in the group. Local education and neighborhood-improvement organizations tend to be dominated by women. The few men involved in neighborhood organizations participate in educational and business organizations but not on a grand scale. Only one economic dominant belongs to a neighborhood organization.

Data were also obtained on the social club memberships of the respondents. Even though such clubs cannot be termed quasi-political in Lane's terminology, they do serve as convenient settings for politically oriented discussions and would fall under the "other" category. One Atlantan underlined the importance of these clubs in his remark that "more decisions that have a large impact on Atlanta are made over the tables of the Capitol City Club than anywhere else." While such a statement is a gross exaggeration and oversimplification, there is no question that political matters are discussed in these surroundings. The Capitol City Club, the Piedmont Driving Club, and the Atlanta Athletic Club are usually considered the most prestigious.

In conformity with expectations, those actors with higher social status—the attributed influentials and the economic dominants—have the highest rates of membership in social clubs. For government officials and civic staffers, the division between those with no memberships and those with one or more is almost identical to that between the paid professionals and the lay leaders. Unless they appear as guests, the professionals must rely strictly on nonsocial hours and settings for communication with other influentials. Since professionals see the relevant lay leaders as a matter of course in their work, there is no need to use social clubs for contact. For other influentials, who may or may not be attached to the civic and governmental agencies represented by the professionals, the communications gap may be serious.

Finally, let us consider the figures for state and national organizational memberships and participation. Contrary to other patterns, government officials have significantly higher scores in this category than does any other elite. The reason lies in the increased professionalization of staff personnel and professionally oriented lay leaders. The importance of such memberships for community decision-making lies in the exposure to other points of view that individuals normally receive as members of state and especially national organizations. Such exposure occurs through print and through face-to-face contact at conventions and committee meetings. The effect is frequently to lessen the provincialism of members and to lift them, in the case of Atlanta, above the prevailing norms that may guide public policy-making. Government officials develop a tendency to identify with counterpart units[7] at the national level, which, on the whole, is a broadening experience. In terms of agreement on public policy, such identifications have mixed blessings. Professional allegiance may become highly developed to the point of discouraging co-operation with professionals in other fields.

Economic dominants evidently refrain from participating extensively in extra-community organizations. In part, this behavior can be accounted for by the relatively low status they enjoy in their own hierarchies, compared to that of businessmen in the perceived elite. That is, the latter are more likely to assume extra-community roles as spokesmen and representatives because of their higher structural positions. The absence of professionalism among the economic notables is also a factor, since professionalism breeds in or is bred by the *professional* large-scale organizations of which the prescribed influentials are more likely to be members.

For the most part, the attributed influentials emerge as the most highly politicized in the area of organization activity. The prescribed influentials and economic dominants are less highly politicized; government officials score particularly low in the world of civic organizations.

Interpersonal Contacts

Rendering advice, taking orders, and issuing directives are typical forms of interpersonal contact in decision-making. The people in key positions with whom other people interact influence the effects of communication and, ultimately, decisional outcomes. Knowing the frequency of such interactions helps to determine, not only the rates of differential access to influentials, but also the relative importance that certain "others" in the environment hold for influentials. Interaction is the common medium for exerting interpersonal influence. It is a third measure of politicization.

These interactions may be viewed as comprising a role-set, which in Merton's words is *"that complement of role relationships which persons have by virtue of occupying a particular social* [read political] *status."*[8] For example, the role-set of a city department head in Atlanta includes his relationships to other department heads, the city board, the mayor's office, his subordinates, his professional colleagues, and so forth. Our aim is to reveal the magnitude of the critical components of the role-set for the political status-occupants who are the subjects of our research. The role-set configuration employed here emphasizes the interpersonal relationships between the status-occupants and others who presumably affect policy-making in the community. The institutional and group representatives include officials at the city, county, public school, state, and national levels; political-party leaders; civic leaders; Negro leaders; and labor-union officials. Because of their legally imposed signif-

icance, the presence of various types of government agents in the
role-set is emphasized.

Among all the elites, rates of interaction with assorted
government officials range from frequent contacts with city and
county government officials to few contacts with national government officials, congressmen, and senators (Table 6). Propinquity and simple proportions help to account for part of this
pattern, which does, however, reflect the primary modes of local

**Table 6. Distribution of Frequent Contacts with Institutional
and Group Representatives***

	ATTRIBUTED INFLUENTIALS		PRESCRIBED INFLUENTIALS		ECONOMIC DOMINANTS
	First Level	Second Level	Government Officials	Civic Staff	
Have frequent personal contacts with:					
City officials	95%	69%	92%	77%	47%
County officials	70	55	50	36	16
Public school officials	55	53	42	41	5
State government officials	40	21	33	9	5
National government officials	20	12	17	14	5
Congressmen or senators	45	15	4	14	10
Negro leaders	30	27	29	23	0
Labor-union officials	20	9	17	4	26
Civic leaders (nongovernmental)	90	97	79	86	83
Number	(19)	(32)	(24)	(22)	(19)

*The question read: "How frequently, if at all, do you have personal contacts with, or asso-
ciate with, the following kinds of people?" Alternative replies were "frequently," "occasionally," and "rarely or never."

policy-making: achieving ends through local governmental officials more often than through state and national agents.

Despite this general distribution of interactions, differential
rates are apparent. First-level attributed influentials have more
frequent contacts with city and county officials than do their
second-level counterparts. Government officials hold a similar
edge over civic-staff people. The latter finding is not unexpected;
virtually all government officials are in daily contact with colleagues. There is a different explanation for the secondary attributed influentials' ranking below the top level. A large

number of the second-level personnel are neither so affluent nor so constantly engaged in community decision-making as those in the top level. The two interrelated factors mean that the secondary influentials have fewer opportunities for contact and consequently interact less frequently with government officials than do the top influentials. The economic dominants lag far behind the others, and their interactions tend to be confined to a smaller number of officials.

Although public schools and public school officials are ubiquitous in a modern American community like Atlanta, they do represent a policy area more specialized than that of city and county officials in general. Frequent association with school officials by the five groups is about the same as or slightly under that with city and county officials. Only one of the economic dominants said he associated frequently with such officials. In contrast to contacts with city and county officials, there is little difference between the subdivisions of either the perceived or prescribed elites.

Turning to interactions with officials above the level of local government, we find a mixed picture. High-level attributed influentials and government officials reported the most frequent associations with state officials. Some members of the former are intimately connected with occupants of high elective offices in Georgia. Hunter's description of the relationships between various Atlanta leaders and the state political office holders and faction leaders[9] still holds true, although the specific characters may have changed. As for government officials, many of them are engaged in programs demanding repeated contacts with state administrative officials. For others such contact is not necessary, so that nearly one-third report only infrequent association. The relatively poor access or perhaps needlessness of access among civic-staff personnel and economic dominants stands out. The policy-oriented activities of the former do not bring them into frequent association with state officials, while the low rate for the latter is a product of their generally less intensive political orientation.

To emphasize the importance of social and political status, there is the pattern of unequal interaction with congressmen or senators. Almost one-half of the top-level influentials reported frequent such associations, while less than 20% of the other elites reported the same. Many first-level influentials contribute heavily to the campaigns of the congressmen and senators. They also serve on various regional and national public and private committees that tend to bring them into contact with national legislators. Finally, as leading businessmen, some of them have economic interests that need the protection or promotion of the national government.

Only 10% of the economic notables reported frequent contacts with congressmen and senators, but a large majority did signify "occasional" contacts (not shown). The reason for this pattern, it appears, is that as representatives of national corporations many of these men are expected to become acquainted with and maintain some contact with the senators and congressmen in the state where they serve. The interests of their corporations are nation-wide; a branch manager in a position to petition a legislator for favors and votes is an asset most national corporations covet.[10]

Finally, association with national government officials, as distinct from congressmen and senators, is quite low among all elites in comparison to association with other institutional representatives. Whether this rate is due to greater inaccessibility of administrative officials or to fewer needs for contact is an unanswered question, though the latter seems more likely.

In addition to reporting their associations with government officials at various levels, the respondents also indicated the frequency of their contacts with three other classes of individual that play diverse roles in Atlanta's decision-making. Rates of interaction with civic leaders, Negro leaders, and labor-union officials are also shown in Table 6.

Let us look first at interactions with labor-union and Negro leaders. Both perceived and prescribed influentials associate more frequently with Negro leaders than with labor-union officials. From this and other data, it can be inferred that Negro leaders are better integrated into the decision-making structure than are labor leaders. One cause is the greater prominence of Negro leadership. Several Negroes preside over well established economic institutions, and a few hold public office or serve on lay committees. As a community in the functional sense, the Negroes are well organized into various types of association, and in voting-block terms the Negroes hold a powerful ace in local elections. In contrast, labor has no representation in public office, although one labor leader does serve on a major lay board.

Labor-union organizations contribute little toward meeting community needs outside the specific area of employer-employee relationships. So far, organized labor does not appear to have acted in a concerted and decisive fashion in local elections. As a result, the caste-encumbered Negroes actually have more opportunity to exert interpersonal influence among attributed and prescribed influentials than do labor leaders. Whether such intercourse is unilateral or primarily bilateral, the basis for exertion of interpersonal influence exists.

In contrast to the other elites, the economic dominants display more contact with labor-union officials than with Negro leaders. Not surprisingly, those economic dominants in firms whose working forces are partially or wholly unionized have more frequent interaction with union officials. However, the largest proportion of infrequent contacts (not shown) also comes from the economic dominants—the opposition of textile firms and other enterprises has effectively prevented unionization of large employee blocks. Consequently, unless their firms are unionized, economic dominants are not likely to have contact with labor union officials, unlike the other elites, which have noneconomic contacts with labor officials. In their relationships to Negro leaders, the economic dominants also reveal a lack of integration; none of them indicated frequent communication and more than two-thirds reported rare, if any, associations. Remove the economic imperatives, and the economic dominants are highly unlikely to associate with these minority-group leaders —labor officials and Negro leaders.

As expected, association with civic leaders is high among all status-groups, although slightly higher for attributed than for prescribed influentials and economic dominants. Knowing that the economic dominants belong to civic organizations and social clubs in large proportions and that, as we shall see, their overt participation in a range of issues is much lower than for the other respondents, it is safe to speculate that contacts between economic notables and civic leaders are less politically oriented than for the other elites. Even though the economic dominants frequently interact with civic leaders in social clubs and in quasi-political civic organizations, they may not use these associations as forums for discussing matters of policy. If they do, they may merely request information from their more active colleagues instead of attempting themselves to exert interpersonal influence.

In general, then, the attributed and prescribed elites are much more politicized than the economic dominants in terms of their role-sets. Upper-level perceived influentials are more politicized than their second-level colleagues, while government officials hold a smaller edge over civic staffers.

Giving Advice

Consultation serves an important function in community decision-making. Proposals may be quickly abandoned or kept under consideration on the strength of a discussion among two or more people. Advice-giving also serves to bridge structural hierarchies. In Atlanta, for example, the managers of the largest department stores often call upon the city traffic engineer for consultation on how to handle their own traffic problems. City and county officials sound out civic leaders for reactions to policy proposals or implementation plans. Civic-staff professionals and governmental planners consult one another on a day-to-day basis. Such acts are power-oriented; they are subsumed under what was earlier called interpersonal influence, and they are an index of politicization.

To ascertain the prevalence of advice-giving among the elites, we asked if they had been asked for advice within the past year on any of nine substantive policy areas. Six of these areas are directly related to the physical development of the community: traffic and parking, rapid transit, urban renewal, water and sewers, physical planning, and airport development. The other three—schools, local elections, and social welfare—are more directly involved with nonphysical issues.

Perhaps the most striking feature of the data in Table 7 is the low incidence of advice-giving among the economic notables. On no topic have more than half of them given advice. The mean scores of advice-giving for the combined problem areas show the other elites far higher than the economic dominants. As the evidence accumulates, we begin to understand two points: why the economic dominants are not perceived as influentials in the community; and how exclusion from governmental or staff offices acts to reduce their involvement.

A second major difference rests in the more extensive advice-giving of high-level compared to second-level attributed influentials and in the almost constant margin of government officials over civic-staff personnel. In the first instance, there is a reaffirmation of the tendency among first-echelon attributed

Table 7. Rates of Advice-Giving in Substantive Areas*

Contacted for Advice on	ATTRIBUTED INFLUENTIALS		PRESCRIBED INFLUENTIALS		ECONOMIC DOMINANTS
	First Level	Second Level	Government Officials	Civic Staff	
Physical problems:					
Planning	90%	79%	100%	72%	20%
Urban renewal	90	72	92	78	45
Traffic and parking	80	75	75	75	50
Rapid transit	60	48	50	45	20
Water and sewers	60	42	63	37	20
Airport development	55	42	50	28	30
Nonphysical problems:					
Schools	85%	75%	84%	81%	50%
Local elections	75	57	71	72	45
Social welfare	60	48	71	63	50
Number	(20)	(33)	(24)	(22)	(20)
Mean Score	73%	60%	73%	61%	37%

*Based on this question: "Now we would like to ask you a question about giving advice on different kinds of subjects in community affairs. First, has anyone come to you within the past year for advice on what can or should be done in regard to any of the subjects indicated below?"

influentials to have more general interests, while those in the second stratum prefer more specialized endeavors. The difference between government officials and civic staffers results from the specific issue-areas presented. All the topics dealing with physical development constitute major governmental problems into which a majority of government officials are likely to be drawn in one way or another.

The prospect of being consulted for advice appears to be related to the generality or specificity of the substantive arena too. Notice that planning, schools, and urban renewal are topics for advice-giving much more frequently than the more specialized areas of water and sewers, rapid transit, and airport development. Then, too, the more general topics are usually more visible and generate more public interest. Government officials tend to rank comparatively better than the other elites in the more specialized and less publicized substantive issue-areas. In terms of all the problem areas, the more generalized ones have, for the most part, the highest incidence of advice-giving. They are the most salient for the actors surveyed here.

These findings prepare us for visualizing varying types of structure according to the policy area under investigation. Not to be overlooked in this connection is the finding that prescribed and attributed influentials are about equally likely to serve as advice-givers (according to mean scores), despite the many differences between them, especially in socio-economic status. Using advice-giving as an index of the scope of a given policy area suggests that an area may involve roughly the same *proportions* of attributed and prescribed influentials, but that the sheer numbers of such participants vary considerably from one issue-area to another.

To learn more about advice-giving patterns, we asked all respondents in the formal interviews for the names of the first three people they would contact within each of the substantive areas if they wanted some advice. Of interest here is the frequency with which the status-occupants are named. It was assumed that the names offered by all the respondents were of sufficient importance to warrant tabulation, although some people named more than others. Starting the count with those most often named, all persons mentioned in the cumulative total reaching 75% (or the nearest total that did not exceed 75%) of all designations in any substantive area were considered as identifiable advice-givers. It should be noted that designations were universally by name, not position. Usually the name was mentioned with an ease and familiarity that bespoke more than "public knowledge" of the person mentioned.

One of the remarkable results of this question was that the members of the attributed and prescribed elites constituted the overwhelming majority of those most frequently named, even though the respondents were free to cite any people they chose. Significantly, only one economic dominant made the ranks of potential advice-givers. Table 8 presents a closer look at the composition of the elect, according to substantive area.

These figures conceal two important points. First, those attributed influentials named as sources of advice were more often than not holders of elective or appointive governmental positions. The two named for airports were the mayor and the chairman of the aldermanic board's aviation committee. Similarly, those named for schools included the superintendents of the Atlanta and Fulton County school systems and the chairman of the city's board of education. The prescribed influentials

Table 8. Those Frequently Designated as Advice-Givers in Issue-Areas

	NUMBER OF:	
	Attributed Influentials	Prescribed Influentials
Airport development	2	0
Water and sewers	1	2
Social welfare	7	4
Urban renewal	4	4
Traffic and parking	1	3
Rapid transit	0	1
Schools	4	0
Local elections	8	2
Planning, zoning, land use	4	4

named were also most often government officials. Those two named for water and sewers, for example, were the city water-works manager and the city chief of construction. For urban renewal, the four prescribed influentials included the urban renewal director, the executive director of the Atlanta Housing Authority, the head of the Citizens Advisory Committee on Urban Renewal, and the director of the Metropolitan Planning Commission.

A second point is that often one or two people received a great plurality of the votes cast. For example, the water-works manager garnered 81 of the 175 designations in that area, and the mayor received 44 of the 183 votes for local elections. Third, a few people were mentioned frequently in connection with more than one issue-area. Again governmental position is important. Of the two prescribed influentials receiving multiple designations, both were public administrators. Five of the six attributed influentials so designated held ranking positions—three elective and two in lay offices.

The importance of these findings is twofold. They indicate, first, the access perceived and prescribed influentials have to recognized sources of advice in the community. Second, they are an indirect measure of politicization and visibility. Most people had little or no trouble citing by name those linked to particular policy areas. The special visibility of incumbents of official positions, both governmental and civic, is important because it suggests that these people serve the function of gate-keepers to information and advice in these areas.

Issue Involvement

During the period of this study, a number of public issues were current or concluded in the Atlanta area. In the next two chapters, three of them are treated in detail. What we wish to do here is to present some gross indices of overt participation in these issues. Power, it will be recalled, requires a degree of manifest behavior that is intentionally designed to influence the outcome of an issue. The higher the level of involvement in an issue, the more power-oriented is the behavior.

The first set of data comes from questions about specific levels of involvement in three issues that were in early stages of development: consolidation of city and county schools, urban renewal, and home rule. Members of the elites were classified into high and low levels of involvement on the basis of their reported activities.

Three main impressions emerge from the distributions in Table 9. First, the economic dominants rank far below the other status-groups on each issue. Where they are involved at all, it is most probably at the medium or "talking" level rather than at the persuasive and energetic stage. Second, the first-stratum attributed influentials score decidedly higher than the other actors on two of the three issues. Only on urban renewal are they challenged by others, and here the figures are nearly equal for all groups except the economic dominants. Finally, the differences between the two subdivisions of the perceived elite, unlike those within the prescribed group, are rather striking in regard to consolidation of schools and home rule. First-level members were considerably more involved than those of the second level. Greatly contributing to this variation is the fact that more issue specialists are found in the ranks of the secondary reputed influentials than in the top level. On a *range* of issues, therefore, they are not likely to appear as activists so frequently as the top influentials.

Looking at each issue separately, the probable reasons for different levels of activity can be discerned. At the time of the research, the question of consolidating the schools was in the preliminary or study stage. A lay committee, appointed by public officials, had been formed under the chairmanship of a

Table 9. Level of Involvement* in Three Fledgeling Issues

Issue and Level of Involvement	ATTRIBUTED INFLUENTIALS		PRESCRIBED INFLUENTIALS		ECONOMIC DOMINANTS
	First Level	Second Level	Government Officials	Civic Staff	
Consolidation of schools					
Low	60%	79%	84%	91%	100%
High	40	21	16	8	0
Urban renewal					
Low	40	33	33	31	84
High	60	67	67	68	16
Home rule					
Low	40	63	63	55	95
High	60	36	37	45	5
Number	(20)	(33)	(24)	(22)	(19)

*A person was classified as highly involved if he used either of these alternatives: "I have become very much concerned and have tried to influence my friends and acquaintances one way or another whenever the subject came up"; "I have felt the decision was very important and have become actively engaged in seeking support for the position I hold by making special calls on individuals, writing letters, talking to officials and influential people, speaking to groups, or some other means of seeking to affect the outcome." He was considered to have low involvement if he used either of these two responses: "I have not been concerned one way or another and have pretty much remained on the sidelines"; "I have become quite interested and have discussed the subject on many occasions with friends and acquaintances."

second-stratum attributed influential. It was a recent issue in terms of its saliency for the community. The data definitely indicate that, at the initiating stage of this issue, the attributed influentials were more highly involved than the prescribed influentials. That the economic dominants had no high-level participants underscores their exclusion from a substantive area of vital concern to the community.

Home rule has been a latent, periodically manifest, issue in Atlanta for several years. Mayor Hartsfield and other officials have led the way in persuading and demanding of the state legislature a measure of home rule for the city. Since the metropolis is suspect in the legislature, however, these pleas have gone unheeded. Still the issue is brought to the fore from time to time. Once again, the top-level attributed influentials have clearly been more deeply involved in this issue. Civic-staff personnel are the second most highly involved elite. Some of them are motivated to work for home rule by a creed of good government and reform. Others, mainly the professionals, are involved because their boards of directors oppose the specific form of home rule proposed.

The final issue, urban renewal, stands unique among the three because concrete action had been taken on the subject. Much of the planning stage had passed, preliminary money had been allocated by the national and local governments, and specialized personnel were devoting full working hours to it. It comes as no surprise that the highest level of involvement for each status-grouping was achieved in this issue-area. Ordinarily the more extensive decision-making becomes, the greater the number of participants. As we shall see in a later chapter, the structure for urban renewal has subsequently undergone further enlargement, and critical decisions are still being made.

Two other issues, each of great importance, were resolved during the time of our research. Although they will be treated in more detail in a subsequent chapter, a glance at them now will illuminate differential participation among elites. The first issue is that of a gigantic ($87 million) omnibus bond issue sponsored jointly by Atlanta and Fulton County. Table 10 in-

Table 10. Activity Level for an Omnibus Bond Issue

	ATTRIBUTED INFLUENTIALS		PRESCRIBED INFLUENTIALS		ECONOMIC DOMINANTS
	First Level	Second Level	Government Officials	Civic Staff	
Activity Level					
None	30%	42%	8%	14%	83%
Only campaigned	20	15	33	23	0
Other activities	50	42	59	63	17
Total	100%	99%	100%	100%	100%
Number	(20)	(33)	(24)	(22)	(19)

dicates, in rough fashion, the degree of participation among the different elites according to whether they had done nothing, had merely campaigned for or against the proposal, or had performed other activities involving greater commitments of time and energy. These last included serving on committees, talking to people on the committees, and appearing before the committees.

The most outstanding finding is the virtual absence of

participation by the economic notables. Despite the fact that this bond program was highly significant in light of the financial burdens imposed on the community and in terms of the city's physical growth, the economic dominants played almost no positive role, not even to the point of campaigning for or against the program's passage. As the figures show, the prescribed influentials in this instance were more active than the attributed influentials. Actually most of that margin lies in the fact that the prescribed influentials, especially the government officials, appeared before the committees to present testimony.

The 1957 general mayoralty election is the second major issue. Activity level was divided into nonparticipation; common, minimal participation; and the more unusual, policy-involved activities. Into the second category fall the activities of speaking to friends and urging members of organizations to vote. Financial contributions, deciding campaign strategy, helping in publicity, giving public endorsement, and helping to formulate a platform form the third category.

As a simple index, the data in Table 11 reveal a different sort of pattern from that for the bond issue. For the more ordinary types of activity, the attributed influentials and economic dominants now rank highest. That government officials belong

Table 11. Activity Level in a Mayoralty Election

	ATTRIBUTED INFLUENTIALS		PRESCRIBED INFLUENTIALS		ECONOMIC DOMINANTS
	First Level	Second Level	Government Officials	Civic Staff	
Activity Level					
None	5%*	9%	21%	14%	5%
Minimal	85	91	75	73	95
Maximal	55	48	5	20	40
Number	(20)	(33)	(24)	(22)	(19)

*Percentages do not total 100% because of overlap between minimal and maximal activities.

to fewer organizations accounts for their relatively poor showing in minimal activities. Another factor is that seven of the government officials serve Fulton County, and most of them prefer to remain aloof from city political elections. The good showing of the economic dominants stems from participation that proved uncostly for them despite their relative unpoliticized nature. It was uncostly because their social groups were predominantly in favor of candidate Mayor Hartsfield, and no conflict with peers was involved in the choice.

Not surprisingly, the attributed influentials lead the way in maximal activities, followed by the economic dominants. As we shall see later, the major reason the economic dominants score rather well is that two-fifths of them contributed financially to Hartsfield's campaign. That 21% of the government officials performed no activities in regard to the election is not surprising since county officials stayed out of the contest.

As with most other measures of politicization, the economic dominants trail the other elites in most realms of issue-involvement. Both the perceived and prescribed elites show moderate to high politicization. Perceived influentials of high rank fare particularly well by these measures.

Summary

Four conclusions stand out in the findings presented in this chapter. First, approximately one-fourth of the attributed influentials are politicized to the point of holding a major governmental position in the community. Another fourth presently hold minor governmental positions, and about one-fifth more have held offices in the past, so that nearly 70% of the attributed influentials are highly politicized in this respect. There is thus a moderate degree of integration between the upper echelons of the legal government structure and the attributed power structure in the community.

Second, the economic dominants have a *relatively* low state of politicization on virtually every measure used. They do not hold public offices. Their rates of participation are lower than those of the other elites. Only in the civic-organization field do the economic dominants approach the other elites in terms of activity.

Third, the attributed and prescribed influentials are almost universally highly politicized, both in absolute terms and when compared with the economic dominants and Atlanta residents in general. Because of the positions that most prescribed influentials hold, this orientation is not unexpected for them. Because, however, of the "reputational" nature of the attributed influentials' political prowess (although we may exclude those who hold major governmental posts), high politicization need not have followed. Yet, not only were they highly politicized, but those accorded the highest status were more politicized than those with lower status.

' Fourth, it should be noted that politicization takes different forms among the perceived and prescribed influentials and also within these two groups. The attributed influentials and civic staffers tend to participate more heavily in politically oriented local organizations than do government officials. Although there are some exceptions, first-level attributed influentials and government officials tend to have more frequent contacts with various types of political actors both in and out of the community. Similarly, these two groups consistently outdistance the second-level influentials and the civic staffers in rendering advice. The extent to which government officials in the prescribed and perceived elites are sought for counsel on substantive issue-areas is also significant. In involvement in specific issues, the first-stratum attributed influentials clearly outrank the other groups on two out of three fledgeling issues. On the other hand, the prescribed influentials had fewer nonparticipants in one fully developed issue—the bond program—but more in the mayoralty election.

NOTES

1. The place of administrators in local decision-making is treated specifically in M. Kent Jennings, "Public Administrators and Community Decision Making," *Administrative Science Quarterly,* VIII (June, 1963), 18-43.
2. Many investigations using the reputational approach point toward less of this type of politicization among the perceived elite. See a compilation in William V. D'Antonio, *et al.,* "Institutional and Occupational Representation in Eleven Community Influence Systems," *American Sociological Review,* XXVI (June, 1961), 440-6. Other efforts have produced results more in line with the Atlanta findings: for example, Robert O. Schulze and Leonard U. Blumberg, "The Determination of Local Power Elites," *American Journal of Sociology,* LXV (January, 1960), 401.
3. Robert E. Lane, *Political Life: Why People Get Involved in Politics* (New York: The Free Press of Glencoe, 1959), p. 79.
4. Floyd Hunter, *Community Power Structure* (Chapel Hill: University of North Carolina Press, 1953), pp. 85-6.
5. Other Atlanta quasi-political organizations employ similar techniques, and their operations can be similarly analyzed, *mutatis mutandis.* The conceptual terms that apply to this phase of the political process at higher governmental levels are also applicable at the community level, that is,

overlapping memberships, differential access, alliances, defensive advantage, expansion of the public, and so forth. Cf. David Truman, *The Governmental Process* (New York: Alfred A. Knopf, Inc., 1958), especially chaps. 11 and 12.

6. For national rates of participation in organizations see Lane, *op. cit.*, p. 78; and Charles R. Wright and Herbert Hyman, "Voluntary Association Memberships of American Adults: Evidence from National Sample Surveys," *American Sociological Review*, XXIII (June, 1958), 284-94.

7. Herbert A. Simon, Donald W. Smithburg, and Victor A. Thompson propound the notion of counterpart units and the organizational problems involved in *Public Administration* (New York: Alfred A. Knopf, Inc., 1950), chaps. 3 and 4.

8. Robert K. Merton, "Reference Groups and Social Structure," in his *Social Theory and Social Structure* (rev. and enlarged ed.; New York: The Free Press of Glencoe, 1957), p. 369. The concept of "role-set" closely resembles formulations of focal position and counterposition in Neal Gross, Ward S. Mason, and Alexander McEachern, *Explorations in Role Analysis: Studies of the School Superintendency Roles* (New York: John Wiley & Sons, Inc., 1958), pp. 48-56.

9. Hunter, *op cit.*, chap. 4.

10. Interaction with "political party leaders" was uniformly low among all elites.

5

THE

SCOPE OF

POLITICIZED ROLES

O NE WRITER HAS APPROACHED the community decision-making process as a conglomeration of games. Norton E. Long argues that

> the structured group activities that coexist in a particular territorial system can be looked at as games. These games provide the players with a set of goals that give them a sense of success or failure. They provide them determinate roles and calculable strategies and tactics. In addition, they provide the players with an elite and general public that is in varying degrees able to tell the score. . . .

> Looked at this way, in the territorial system there is a political game, a banking game, a contracting game, a newspaper game, a civic organization game, an ecclesiastical game, and many others.[1]

In this chapter, we focus on the scope of games or issues engaged in by the elites. More specifically, attention is directed to the frequency and level of participation in different games. We explore participation in three *major* games (or arenas) and

ernmental game, compared to 40% who gave examples of fund-raising games, and only 28% who participated in private games. This breakdown tends to corroborate the view that issues in the governmental arena constitute the most decisive ones for the community.

Only 4% reported involvement in no issues or projects. It is significant, however, that this percentage came entirely from the ranks of the economic dominants. Viewing this category as a whole, one-fifth (of a total of nineteen) could recall no issue, problem, or project of any consequence in which they had engaged over the previous two or three years. Such uninvolvement is consistent with our discussion of the politicization of economic dominants in the previous chapter.

Other significant findings are buried in the over-all distribution. For example, some players concentrated their energy in one major sphere. Once more, the economic dominants stand out in marked contrast to the others. They are the only respondents who specialized in private issues (11%). Most of these activities were rather innocuous projects like Junior Achievement Awards and minor cultural or welfare projects. Only the two or three issues that involved the attraction of new businesses to Atlanta could be said to have major effects on the community at large.

Another 21% of the economic dominants concentrated on fund-raising ventures. The only other group with any concentration in this arena is the second-level perceived influentials, 17% of whom listed fund-raising projects. Participation in fund-raising games among the economic dominants usually excludes behavior other than that explicitly required to ensure the co-operation of the individual's firm. On the other hand, the second-level perceived influentials tend to take part in planning, organizing, making contact with other people, publicity, and other phases as well.

Fifteen per cent of the economic notables listed a combination of private and fund-raising games. Altogether, nearly one-half of the economic notables cited issues exclusively in these two nongovernmental spheres. Only small proportions of the other elites had similar profiles (see Table 12).

Concentration in private and fund-raising games usually represents only modest commitment to community service. In their study of mobile big businessmen at the community level, Warner and Abegglen make the following observation about the business-centered world of their subjects:

This focusing on the business career extends to those activities that ostensibly lie somewhat outside the immediate business realm, for example, running the finance drive for the Red Cross, YMCA, or Community Chest; for such activities are a definite part of a man's job as an executive and are frequently undertaken on explicit or implicit instructions from his company.[6]

Most of the economic dominants in Atlanta and certainly those employed by nonlocal firms fit this description. Since they do not want to become involved in issues that are controversial and since they believe at the same time that they should partici-

Table 12. Engagement in Decision-Making Arenas

	ATTRIBUTED INFLUENTIALS		PRESCRIBED INFLUENTIALS		ECONOMIC DOMINANTS
Type of Major Arena	First Level	Second Level	Government Officials	Civic Staff	
Only government	33%	47%	73%	41%	5%
Government combined with fund-raising or private	55	33	27	45	27
Only fund-raising and/or private	11	20	0	14	47
None	0	0	0	0	21
Total	99%	100%	100%	100%	100%
Number	(18)	(30)	(22)	(22)	(19)

pate somehow, they enter relatively uncontroversial and painless private or fund-raising projects that serve as functional substitutes for more decisive activity. Thus, even among the economic dominants who did identify issues in which they had participated over the past two or three years, only one specialized in the arena that ordinarily offers the highest stakes—the legal-governmental.

With the exception of the economic dominants, each elite has a moderate to high concentration of specialization in the governmental game. Within the other four classes, there is considerable variation—from 33% and 47% respectively for the first- and second-level attributed influentials to 73% and 41% respectively for government officials and civic staffers. Perhaps the most noteworthy fact is that approximately three-fourths of the government officials restrict their scopes to the legal arena. Given the vocational environment and professional requirements among government officials, this concentration is not surprising. The involvement of minor elective officials and the minor lay chairmen in the governmental arena, however, evidently serves to focus their major issue-involvements too.

There are two more explicit reasons why government officials, both professional and nonprofessional, specialize so intensely. First, the vocational interests and demands on the time of those in governmental positions serve to deter them from seeking participation in other games. Many of these actors become completely absorbed in their work and have neither time nor interest to expand their major arenas. Second, the very positions they occupy tend to limit their access to other institutional programs. Officials in fund-raising and private games often do not seek the support of government officials because such support is not necessary. The typical government professional, for example, does not have the social status to achieve a ranking position in any of the various city-wide welfare drives.

Between one-third and one-half of the attributed influentials and the civic staffers concentrate on the governmental arena. What factors distinguish them from their fellows who do not have such a concentration? A plausible hypothesis for the attributed influentials is that the legal-game specialists occupy governmental positions, while those not specializing in this game do not. The data support this hypothesis. Of those specializing in the governmental game (N=20), 70% hold government positions. Among those who do not show such specialization (N=28), only 42% hold government positions. Since the attributed influentials are, almost without exception, people of high social status, the likelihood that they are excluded from other major arenas seems slight. Rather, their concentration is probably a product of interest and time commitments.

To explain why approximately two-fifths of the civic staffers concentrate on the legal game requires a different approach, since only one of them occupies a minor government post. One possible explanation lies in the fact that four of the six women in the civic-staff grouping concentrate on governmental issues. On the other hand, only five of the sixteen men specialize in such activity. Women in this group, then, are more prone to emphasize the governmental game than are men. This finding is not surprising, since most of these women are associated with educational or voting organizations. For the men who specialize in this game, no easy explanation is apparent. One possibility, however, is suggested by the fact that four of the eight full-fledged, staff professionals, compared to only one of the eight nonprofessionals show such specialization. It may be, as with the professional government officials, that the demands of their positions promote a focus on government-oriented issues among the truly professional civic-staff men.

Many of the status-occupants (45%) identified issues, problems, or projects in more than one major arena. The overwhelming majority of this group combined a governmental game with either a fund-raising or private game (Table 12), thus reconfirming the notion that the governmental game is the most salient for the prescribed and attributed influentials.

One interesting facet of multi-arena engagement is the variations among the elites. Top-level attributed influentials were more apt than their second-level colleagues to cite more than one major type of game. Participation in multiple games seems to affect a person's chances of being perceived as a general leader in the community. That is, as others in the community observe a person exercising influence over the outcomes of multiple games, they come to attribute a general type of influence or leadership to that person. Variation between the two levels of the attributed elite could therefore be a reflection of ability among the higher echelon to exert influence in more than one major arena.

Recalling the specialization of government officials in the governmental game, their relatively low distribution among different forms of game-playing is understandable (Table 12). Civic-staff personnel, however, are not concentrated in one arena. Their positions, if they are full-time professionals, often require participation in more nongovernmental games than do those of government officials. For example, an official with the Chamber of Commerce has to work, not only on substantive public matters like street and traffic control, but also on private projects like business education. A staff role in the Urban League necessitates working with private and social organizations and participation in fund-raising campaigns, as well as involvement in such governmental games as urban renewal and public housing.

The nonprofessional staff role permits and encourages multi-game-playing also. A young vice-president in the mass media thus finds himself in the governmental game of urban renewal and in the fund-raising contest for a Red Cross drive. A department-store vice-president directs the Symphony Guild in a private game, serves on the Traffic and Transportation Commission in the government arena, and works for the United Appeal in a fund-raising contest. A majority of nonprofessional-staff personnel emerge as dilettantes in community decision-making. Their activities in a number of major games serve to reinforce their predilection for and acceptance into the various continuous processes of decision-making.

High and Low Stakes in Major Games

All the games in which the elites perform are not of equal importance; that is, the stakes in some games are higher than in others. By classifying the major issues, projects, and problems the actors reported engaging in over the past two or three years, we can arrive at a rough approximation of the distribution among high-stakes games, low-stakes games, and combinations of both. Ordinarily, if a person exerts influence in a high-stakes game, he is said to be more influential than one who exerts similar influence in a game with low stakes.[7] The working definition for a game of high stakes takes in those contests that involve a relatively large proportion of the general population and those that have a major, widespread impact on the people and institutions in the community. Games with low stakes include those that involve a relatively small proportion of the general population and those that have a minor, segmental impact on the people and institutions of the community. Examples of the former type range from political elections and bond issues to traffic problems, urban renewal, and the major welfare drive of the community. Instances of the latter type include minor welfare drives, surveys of aged people's needs, voter registration, and regulations on motor scooter use.[8]

As demonstrated in Table 13, the tendency is for status-holders to compete in both high-stakes and low-stakes games. Our definitions do not imply that the players themselves do not identify the prizes of all the games in which they participate as valuable. In terms of impact on the community or degree of involvement by the community as a whole, however, the games are of varying worth. Only the economic dominants depart from the tendency to mix both kinds—a majority of them concentrate on issues of low stakes (Table 13). The relatively low proportion

Table 13. Participation in Issues of Varying Stakes

	ATTRIBUTED INFLUENTIALS		PRESCRIBED INFLUENTIALS		ECONOMIC DOMINANTS
Level of Stakes Involved	First Level	Second Level	Government Officials	Civic Staff	
Only low	17%	20%	14%	14%	58%*
Only high	33	7	14	23	0
Both low and high	50	73	73	64	42
Total	100%	100%	101%	101%	100%
Number	(18)	(30)	(22)	(22)	(19)
Percentage in at least one high-stakes issue	83	80	87	87	42

*Includes five who were unable to cite any issues in which they had participated.

of first-level attributed influentials competing in combinations is compensated for by frequency of their participation in high-stakes games. Because of their high status, they may be able to select more freely the arenas in which they act—in contrast to the prescribed influentials, who must respond to the requirements of their positions, or to the second-level attributed influentials, who may be subject to pressures from higher-level influentials to play in games of wide-ranging values.

An Atlanta planner, for example, named as two of his biggest recent projects his work on a large bond issue and the mapping of streets in the city. The former was obviously more important to the community as a whole and involved many more actors than does the latter project, which was primarily a technical exercise whose policy implications are yet to be revealed and whose execution required not more than a handful of people. An educational official in Fulton County suggested a sizable school bond issue and his service on the Young Americans centennial building program as two of his major projects. Again, the former must be counted more significant than the latter. Yet this man's strategic position in the community and his professional concern with the community's youth make him an attractive candidate for the latter project. In fact, he may not be able to avoid such enterprises, even if he has no interest in them.

The various tangential relations to which the attributed and prescribed influentials are parties probably preclude their dissociation from low-stakes games. Such games serve to establish and maintain the personal influence that is the basis for their participation in more momentous games. The resulting ego-involvement has the effect of making these low-stakes games quite important to the actors themselves, although for the community as a whole the consequences may be comparatively minor.

All of the exclusively high-stakes contestants engaged in at least one governmental issue or project, and 85% of those who listed both high- and low-stakes games included a governmental game, while the rest were divided among fund-raising and private games. Only 45% of the exclusively low-stakes contestants listed a governmental game. It seems, therefore, that the more a person contests for valuable stakes, the more likely he is to include the governmental arena in his repertory.

The Scope of Advice-Giving

Because the governmental sphere in general appears to be the most crucial one in community policy-making, an intriguing question arises: To what extent do the political elites of Atlanta participate in a variety of subgames within the broad governmental framework? Do they tend to have low or high scopes of participation in local decision-making? Are their role-enactments limited to one or two issue-areas, or do they include many?

The first measure of role-scope in the governmental game emanates from the pattern of advice-giving in a number of substantive policy areas (reported in another context in Chapter 4). These areas include local elections, schools, traffic and parking, rapid transit, urban renewal, airport facilities, water and sewers, social welfare, and physical planning for development and growth. While it is evident that some of these topics are more common to all groups than are others (local elections for example), it is also clear that the very diversification and specialization of roles permits us to classify some of the actors as having higher scopes than others.

Those respondents who had given recent advice in four or fewer issue-areas were considered to have low scopes, and those reporting between five and nine issue-areas were considered to have high scopes. Of the forty-three respondents with low scopes, four reported giving no advice on any of the nine subjects, and another half-dozen named only one. By a strict definition of monomorphism,[9] only a handful of the actors thus qualify as pure types, using this measure. Given the elite nature of all the status groups, however, this finding is not unexpected. Most significant of the entries in Table 14 is the

Table 14. Scope of Influence Areas Measured by Advice-Giving

	ATTRIBUTED INFLUENTIALS		PRESCRIBED INFLUENTIALS		ECONOMIC DOMINANTS
Scope	First Level	Second Level	Government Officials	Civic Staff	
Low (0-4 areas)	20%	36%	12%	41%	70%
High (7-9 areas)	80	64	88	59	30
Total	100%	100%	100%	100%	100%
Number	(20)	(33)	(24)	(22)	(20)
Average number of areas	6.5	5.5	6.5	5.3	3.2

high percentage of economic dominants among the low dispersives, that is, people with narrow role-scopes. Three of them said they had given advice in no area. This picture is consistent with previous evidence demonstrating the relatively low politicization of the economic dominants.

At the other extreme are seventy-six actors who are highly dispersed among specific issue-areas; they reported participation in a large proportion of the specific games listed. Sixteen claimed they had given advice on all nine policy areas—they have extremely high scopes. The sixteen included five government officials, one civic staffer, four second-level attributed influentials, six first-level attributed influentials, and no economic dominants. Proportionately, the government officials and the top-level attributed influentials contributed most to the extreme dispersives. Seven of the ten attributed influentials who reported giving advice in all nine areas hold governmental positions. We can conclude that there is a high relationship between holding such positions and multiple game-playing—having high scopes—within the governmental arena. Although 51% of all attributed influentials hold governmental positions, the proportion for attributed influentials *with high scopes* is somewhat higher—68%.

Without question, a decided majority of the attributed and prescribed influentials have high scopes of advice-giving. Among the attributed elite, those who are reputed to be the most influential have considerably more high-scope advice-givers. More advice-giving seems to be consonant with a higher reputation for influence. Government officials outrank civic-staff personnel by an even wider margin. The former have a greater "natural" base for rendering advice because of their official positions.

Personal Estimation of Scope in Substantive Areas

In another question designed to help determine the scope of behavior related to political influence, the interviewees were asked to estimate their own influence as "more than most people," "about average," or "less than most people"—in the arenas of school affairs, community recreation, health affairs, social welfare, taxes and community finance, transportation and traffic, community development for orderly growth, and local government in general.[10] Using these self-ratings as actual indices of influence obviously involves the risk of excessive reliance on subjective evaluations. But the self-ratings may be taken as valid indications of each individual's range or scope of issue-involvement. To be certain that a maximum amount of involvement was present in each case, only those ratings of "more influence than most people" were used as signs of high involvement. With this standard, we obtained a range running from high engagement in all eight issues (by two actors) to engagement in no issues (by thirteen actors). Significantly, the latter group included five economic dominants (from a total of twenty), while the other elites were represented by two respondents each.

In contrast to our findings about *advice-giving* in similar areas, the frequencies now cluster more toward the lower end of the continuum. Modesty probably accounts for some of this variation. More significantly, however, the data suggest that giving advice in a policy arena represents a lower magnitude of influence than does a high self-rating. That is, a political actor refers to a concrete situation when he tries to evaluate his influence in a policy arena. For example, when asked about his influence in health affairs, one person commented, "Well, I've served on the hospital board for years and helped build the new hospital so I guess you would have to say I'm pretty influential in that area." Advice-giving, although it does discriminate among the elites, does not necessarily signify extensive involvement in concrete structures.

We classified those who rated themselves as more influential than most people in three or fewer spheres as having low scopes (N=64) and those in from four to eight arenas as having high scopes (N=53). In the resulting distribution, shown in Table 15, the extremes are the top-level attributed influentials on the

Table 15. Scope of Influence Areas Measured by Self-Ratings

Scope	ATTRIBUTED INFLUENTIALS		PRESCRIBED INFLUENTIALS		ECONOMIC DOMINANTS
	First Level	Second Level	Government Officials	Civic Staff	
Low (0-3 areas)	21%	28%	46%	68%	85%
High (4-8 areas)	79	72	54	32	15
Total	100%	100%	100%	100%	100%
Number	(19)	(32)	(24)	(22)	(20)
Average number of areas	4.4	4.2	3.9	3.0	1.9

one hand and the economic dominants on the other. Not only do others attribute widely disparate political influence to these two groups, but they, themselves, make similar evaluations. Because of the strategic institutional positions they hold, their personal predilections for involvement, their interpersonal contacts with others, and the prizes for which they are competing, the high-level attributed influentials are active in a far greater number of policy areas than are the economic notables. This disparity exists despite the marked similarities between these two groups in the social and economic spheres, similarities that some people might expect to insure political similarities as well.

Among the other three elites, the breakdowns reveal that the second-level attributed influentials trail their more highly placed brothers by only a slight margin. Government officials split almost evenly between low-scope and high-scope influence. On the other hand, the civic staffers have a disproportionate figure in the low-scope bracket. The dividing line between government officials and civic-staff personnel with extensive scopes and those with restricted scopes is somewhat similar to that between full-time paid professionals and laymen who have other occupations or pastimes. For example, 60% of the professionals

among the government officials and about 70% of the professional civic-staff personnel fall into the low-scope bracket—while
the corresponding percentages for the nonprofessionals are 40%
and 50% respectively. For the most part, the professionals' nar-
rower focuses can be explained by the demands of their positions,
which inhibit their ability to expand into other issue-areas. Their
roles are more limited to the responsibilities accompanying their
statuses in the particular hierarchies of which they are a part.

Holding government positions is associated with the role-
scopes of the attributed influentials. Sixty-eight per cent of the
twenty-two with high scopes held government positions while
only 42% of the thirty-one with low scopes held such posts.
It is clear that holding goverment positions can also be positively
related to the ranges of significant games in which the actors
perform their roles.

Scope of Activity in Specific Issues

Still another measure of the scope of influence behavior
within the governmental arena can be employed. In Chapter
4, we outlined the differential participation of the elites in three
substantive issues that were not fully developed at the time
of this study. Inspecting overlapping participation among highly
involved actors in these three issues yields another measure of
scope. To distinguish those with high scopes, we noted those
actors who had indicated that the following statement described
their activities on at least two of the issues:

I have felt the decision was very important and have become actively
engaged in seeking support for the positions I hold by making special
calls on individuals, writing letters, talking to officials and influential
people, speaking to groups, or some other means of seeking to affect
the outcome.

Those who checked less positive statements for at least two
issues were classified as having low involvement for present
purposes (see footnote to Table 9, p. 82).

With this rather stringent standard of high involvement,
the numbers of high-scope influentials decrease in comparison
with some of the other measures used. Seventy-five individuals
(64%) registered low involvement; that is, they had put forth

extreme efforts to affect the outcome of no or only one issue. Forty-three (36%) registered extensive scopes; that is, they had exerted great effort in two or three of the issues.

On the basis of previous indices, we would predict that first-level attributed influentials would have the highest scopes and the economic dominants the lowest. As Table 16 reveals,

Table 16. Scope of High Involvement in Three Issues*
Not Fully Developed

Scope by Number of Issues	ATTRIBUTED INFLUENTIALS		PRESCRIBED INFLUENTIALS		ECONOMIC DOMINANTS
	First Level	Second Level	Government Officials	Civic Staff	
Low					
None	30%	24%	25%	18%	74%
One	10	39	38	50	11
High					
Two	30	21	25	23	16
Three	30	15	12	9	0
Total	100%	99%	100%	100%	101%
Number	(20)	(33)	(24)	(22)	(19)
Average number of issues	1.6	1.3	1.2	1.2	.6

*Home rule, school consolidation, and urban renewal (at an early stage).

this prediction is borne out. Even when the operational definition for high scope is quite stringent, more than one-half (60%) of the top-level attributed influentials still meet it. Notice that nearly three-fourths of the economic dominants were highly involved in *none* of the issues, while not one registered high involvement in all three issues. The similarity of response among the other three elites illustrates the restrictions on multiple roles imposed on them by their institutional positions, interests, and abilities. It should be remembered that these three issues were not so fully developed at the time as were many other issues in the community.

There is one final measure of the role-scopes of the status-holders. Two major issues that had recently been resolved were a large bond program and a mayoralty election (mentioned in Chapter 4). In addition, urban renewal developed into a full-blown issue during the time of the study. These issues differ from those used in Table 16 in that they were either completed or at an advanced stage by the time this research ended. More actors may thus be active on the latter issues than on the former.

The extent of overlap, i.e., scope, in these advanced issues serves as our final index to generalized and specialized political behavior.

Using only activities showing maximum involvement[11] as indicators of power acts, we were able to determine overlapping participation. One of the most remarkable findings is the high similarity among the four elites, excluding the economic dominants (Table 17). In contrast to the less mature issues, where the

Table 17. Scope of High Involvement in Three Issues* Fully Developed

Scope by Number of Issues	ATTRIBUTED INFLUENTIALS		PRESCRIBED INFLUENTIALS		ECONOMIC DOMINANTS
	First Level	Second Level	Government Officials	Civic Staff	
Low					
None	15%	6%	4%	18%	42%
One	20	21	25	14	42
High					
Two	30	45	33	41	11
Three	35	27	38	27	5
Total	100%	99%	100%	100%	100%
Number	(20)	(33)	(24)	(22)	(19)
Average number of issues	1.8	1.9	2.0	1.8	.8

*Bond issue, mayoralty campaign, urban renewal (at an advanced stage).

top-level attributed influentials easily surpassed the other elites in involvement, all four groups show about the same levels of engagement in these advanced issues. As issues develop, the number of significant actors expands. The kinds of role and function necessary for carrying a project or issue to full fruition elicit the involvement of actors who may not have been participants at the beginning.

In comparison to the attributed and prescribed influentials, the economic dominants, not unexpectedly, rank quite low. Eighty-four per cent were highly involved in none or only one of the issues. They actually fare as well as they do because of their participation in the mayoralty campaign. As will be noted later, a moderate number of them did make a maximal commitment in terms of contributing money, although they did little else in the campaign.

There are three distinguishing characteristics of the actors who performed power acts in two or three of the three issues. First, a majority of the thirty-two individuals (56%) active in all three issues indicated that they specialized in the governmental arena; they listed all governmental games when asked to give the most important issues in which they had been involved during the previous two or three years. As the role-scopes narrow, the concentration declines to 39%, 30%, and 18% for the two- one-, and no-issue participants, respectively. Specializing in the governmental sphere, then, increases the probability of engaging in power acts in these three major issues.

Second, those with high scopes occupy governmental positions in much greater proportions than do the other status-holders. The percentages run 61%, 41%, 46% and 21% for the four levels of participation. Finally, those who classified themselves as having high influence in a large number of substantive governmental issue-areas also tended to be most active in these three major issues. For instance, 79% of those with high scopes of self-attributed influence in substantive arenas were highly involved in two or three of the advanced issues. Conversely, only 47% of those with low scopes of self-attributed influence were highly involved in two or three of those issues. Specializing in the governmental game, holding governmental positions, and self-attribution of high-scope influence in continuous substantive concerns are, therefore, three conditions accompanying high-scope influence in the three concrete issues that have matured and been partly or wholly resolved.

As with other data presented on role-scopes, analysis of involvement in major issues points toward a configuration of decision-making structures that depends upon the issues or games being observed. On the basis of high-involvement measures alone, to say nothing of differential outcomes, the evidence is against the conclusion that there is a homogenous and pervasive ruling elite in Atlanta. All four subgroups of attributed and prescribed influentials include moderate numbers of people who were highly involved in none or only one major issue. Furthermore, the fact that substantial numbers of each elite actively participated in all three issues is evidence that high scopes are not confined to only one political-status group.

On the other hand, we must also reject the notions that the resolution of major issues entails entirely separate structures or games and that influentials restrict their power acts to only

one major structure at a given time (these issues were all con-
current though at slightly different stages). Rather, as other
data also indicate, various actors do, indeed, participate in a
considerable range of structures, especially in the arena of governmental games. While we can grant the existence of high-
scope influentials in Atlanta, it is clear that they are not
restricted to the top-level attributed influentials. Some prescribed
influentials, even though they do not have the socio-economic
requisites for attributed political status, are able to parlay their
positions and expertise into high role-scopes.

In summary, the material in this chapter adds new weight
to the findings in earlier chapters and provides a new dimension
to the study as well. The high politicization of the attributed
and prescribed elites, compared with that of the economic
notables, was demonstrated again. The importance of governmental games for the former was in marked contrast to their
relative unimportance for the economic dominants. As for
the scope of politicized behavior within the framework of
governmental games, we saw that the economic dominants
scored rather low. Both the prescribed and attributed influentials, however, registered moderate to extensive scopes, with
the first-level attributed influentials and the government officials
outranking the other two subgroups. Holding a governmental
position proved to be a conducive factor in achieving high
scopes among the attributed elite. In terms of sheer scope of
participation, the findings do not warrant a picture of a homogeneous, generalized elite in Atlanta. Nevertheless, some actors
do have extremely extensive role-scopes.

NOTES

1. Norton E. Long, "The Local Community as an Ecology of Games,"
American Journal of Sociology, LXIV (November, 1958), 252-3.

2. Fund-raising is, of course, a special type of private enterprise. It is
treated separately because of its importance in community affairs and because the processes involved tend to differ from those of other private games.

3. Too few studies recognize the significance and appropriateness of
such games for an understanding of community decision-making. A notable
exception is Roscoe C. Martin, Frank J. Munger, *et al.*, *Decisions in Syracuse*
(Bloomington: Indiana University Press, 1961), pp. 238-302.

4. Hunter has been criticized for stressing fund-raising and private

games in his study of Atlanta—*Community Power Structure* (Chapel Hill: University of North Carolina Press, 1953).

5. This assumption on our part is no guarantee that an individual actually exercised power in any issue he cited. Two factors, however, confirm our belief that most of the respondents had actually exerted forms of power. First, the interviewees had to indicate what specific role-behavior they had engaged in for each issue they listed. Virtually all respondents indicated that they had performed three or more of the nine possible acts listed. Second, we had enough acquaintance with many of the issues cited to know that the respondents had, indeed, exercised some type or types of power in the issues they had cited. At least then, the issue-involvements cited are examples of politicization; at most, they are valid indicators of power.

6. W. Lloyd Warner and James C. Abegglen, *Big Business Leaders in America* (New York: Harper & Row, Publishers, 1955), p. 98.

7. As James Robinson writes, "Measuring influence is a combination of gauging the degree of participation in making decisions, the scope of values affected by those decisions, and the extent of the consequences of and the number of persons affected by the decisions." *Congress and Foreign Policy-Making* (Homewood: The Dorsey Press, 1962), p. 13.

8. These admittedly subjective criteria are not infallible. Acquaintance with the community and the history of particular issues, however, served to facilitate the classifications.

9. In this context "monomorphism" means involvement or influence in one issue-area; polymorphism means involvement or influence in multiple areas.

10. The question read, "We know that it is very difficult for anyone to judge how effective he is as far as influencing the actions and opinions of others or in getting certain policies adopted. Even so, it would be helpful if you would try. It may be easier to answer this type of question by selecting specific areas of influence. How would you rate yourself in each of the following areas?"

11. The criteria for high involvement in the bond program and mayoralty election were those activities outlined on pp. 83-4 of chap. 4 and treated in more detail in the following two chapters. Active participation in the urban-renewal issue (after the main research for this study was finished) was determined on the basis of extended research on that issue.

6

DECISION-MAKING ROLES

AND TYPES OF POWER:

IN LESS CONTROVERSIAL AND

MORE ROUTINE ISSUES

THE TWO PRECEDING CHAPTERS demonstrated in aggregate the relative forms and scopes of politicization for the five elites. To focus more specifically on the types of role-enactment and power such politicization includes we must examine specific issues and their resolution. A simple dissection of the decision-making process facilitates such analysis.[1] For purposes of discussion, this process will be divided into five components or steps. First is *initiation of action*. This phase typically involves confrontation of the problem, issue, or project—a first step toward conquering the task at hand.

The second stage is *fixing priorities or allocating certain preferred values*. Bargaining and compromise often attend this stage, although the complete determination of goals by certain actors is by no means precluded. Deciding whether a bond issue

107

will contain an allocation for street improvements rather than for extension of sewer lines is an example of fixing priorities. The third step is *utilizing resources for gaining acceptance of chosen alternatives.* This process is normally called promoting or campaigning. Although appeals to the public are often made, this need not be the case. Such varied activities as persuading the city council to adopt a zoning ordinance or urging the voters to elect John Brown are illustrations of this stage.

A fourth segment is *legitimation,* which occurs when any body with recognized and explicit authority (in the legal sense or resting on custom and obedience to folkways and mores) takes action to resolve formally the issue or settle the problem. The voters, for example, legitimate when they decide, by casting their ballots, who will hold office in the ensuing term. Finally, *implementation* is involved in many decision-making sequences. Spending the money authorized under an appropriations bill is one type of implementation, as is the condemnation of housing for urban-renewal purposes.

These five steps need not necessarily occur in chronological order, although they often do in the resolution of specific issues. Nor are they necessarily confined to clearly delimited periods of time in the decision-making process. In fact, various stages in the total process may be repeated several times. Nevertheless, most issues do seem to break down broadly into these major phases, although certain phases may be more important in some issues than in others. We may think of the participation in these phases by actors as role-activities, role-enactments, or decision-making roles.

In addition to these role-activities, we are also interested in specifying the types of power act that the actors do or do not perform on given issues. For the most part, the following analysis is confined to designating *positive, filter,* and *veto* forms of power. It will be recalled that positive power is M's achievement of outcome X; that veto power occurs when M prevents T from achieving outcome X where X represents a change in the *status quo;* and that filter power is A's success in regulating or manipulating communication (information) to M who is able to achieve or prevent outcome X.

Analytically then, we have constructed a mental matrix consisting of role-enactments in the decision-making process cut across by dimensions of power. We shall now proceed to examine some specific issues that have arisen in Atlanta in the light of this matrix. In addition to elucidating the relationship between status and decision-making roles, our analysis will also yield insights into the general structure of policy-making in Atlanta. The presence of all the matrix elements for any given issue is not necessary to reveal the role-activities and exercise of power among the actors under study.[2] In the following case studies, these subscripts are used to designate political status classification: a—attributed influential; p—prescribed influential; e—economic dominant. Those who belong to none of the status-groups are not designated by a subscript.

Examples of Veto Power

Some issues never proceed beyond the initial phase, or they may languish in that phase for years before finally coming under the closer scrutiny of Atlanta's decision-makers, whether governmental or nongovernmental. The ability to keep issues latent is one index of veto power.[3] The vetoers may not be able to achieve their own ultimate goals, but they can block the goal-attainment of other actors. For our purposes, the use of the term "veto power" is restricted to its negative connotation, that is, as a defensive maneuver designed to prevent change in the *status quo*.

The issue of whether to fluoridate Atlanta's water supply offers an illustration both of veto power and of curtailed development of the decision-making process. For several years, the Junior Chamber of Commerce had campaigned for fluoridation. Successive Junior Chamber presidents attempted to provide continuity in the attempt. One of them recounted at the time of this study that the Junior Chamber had secured the support of the local medical and dental associations, the Women's Chamber of Commerce, most of the PTA organizations in the area, and various neighborhood councils and clubs. There seemed to be sufficient support on the board of aldermen to adopt fluoridation if the issue could be brought before it. Finally, the local press had supported the cause for a number of years through its editorial columns. During the course of one year, an average of one editorial a month in favor of fluoridation appeared in the *Atlanta Constitution*.

Despite all this support, however, the campaign for fluorida-

tion had never become widespread in the community. In terms
of our decision-making phases, this issue had progressed through
the initiation, allocation, and promotional stages—but on a scale
so minuscule that the probabilities of eventual legitimation and
implementation were slight. The two major causes for the
proponents' failure lay in indifference and hostility. The primary opposition for many years came from Mayor Hartsfield$_a$,
a vociferous opponent of fluoridation, and city water-department
head, Paul Weir$_p$. The mayor's refusal to approve fluoridation
effectively kept the board of aldermen from taking action on it.
Weir was the one professional government official whose backing was logically the most needed to ensure the adoption of
fluoridation. In effect, these two men were exercising a veto
against placing the issue on the official agenda of community
concerns.

Hartsfield$_a$ and Weir$_p$ used various devices to veto fluoridation. They claimed that, as a health measure, fluoridation should
be paid for by the county, since the county, under the Plan of
Improvement, has charge of all health functions for Atlanta
and Fulton County. On the other hand, county officials have
traditionally argued that, as an issue dealing primarily with
water, an area of city responsibility, fluoridation should be
financed by the city. Mayor Hartsfield$_a$ also noted, in the stress
of a mayoralty race, that he would approve fluoridation if an
impartial study by the American Medical Association could
prove that the process was beneficial. After this declaration, the
mayor was questioned by proponents of fluoridation, who asked
him if he intended to imply that some studies were partial and
others impartial. His reply indicated that he had, indeed, hedged
his declaration of potential support.

Although evasion and hostility partially account for the
suppression of the pro-fluoridation drive, indifference, passivity,
and conflict among community influentials also helped to veto
the innovation. During the structured interviews, all respondents were asked for their opinions of fluoridation; answers were
given on the basis of five choices, ranging from "strongly approve" to "strongly disapprove." Approximately 60% of both
the attributed and prescribed influentials replied that they
"strongly approved" or "approved" of fluoridation, while the
remaining 40% either were "undecided," "disapproved," or

"strongly disapproved." This division of opinion reveals a basic weakness in the movement for fluoridation. Although there are exceptions, major policy innovations in Atlanta usually are based on near unanimity among community influentials. If wide diversity of opinion exists, the proposed project is likely to flounder or to be delayed for a long period of time. No forceful combination of key influentials, either attributed or prescribed, had been willing to attempt a positive act of power on the fluoridation issue. The net result was a veto of the prolonged but weak efforts of the Junior Chamber of Commerce.[4]

As we have suggested, the best examples of veto power are those defensive maneuvers designed to protect the *status quo*. The next example comes from a nongovernmental arena but one that lies at the heart of much civic enterprise—social welfare activities. What makes this case especially compelling is that it also involved—indeed focused on—the long-lived problem of race relations.

The Community Chest drive (now United Appeal) is the biggest annual social welfare fund-raising project in Atlanta and distributes its receipts among more than fifty social-service agencies in a three-county area. Among the recipients is the forty-year-old Atlanta Urban League, an organization whose major purpose is to provide social and economic aid for Negroes. In 1956, the Community Chest came under the fire of "states' rights" groups in Georgia for including the Urban League in its membership. The segregationists charged the League with promoting racial strife and tension and concluded that it should be excluded from the welfare drive's beneficiaries. Tackling the Community Chest was striking at one of the time-honored civic activities in Atlanta. Traditionally, the leaders of the Community Chest have come from some of the city's most prominent economic firms. Furthermore, attacking the Urban League represented criticism of one institutionalized device for accommodation between the races. An example of significant support for the Urban League appeared in the formal interview data. When asked to indicate their feelings about Atlanta's Urban League on a five-point scale running from "strongly approve" to "strongly disapprove," three-fourths or more of each group of attributed or prescribed influentials replied that they strongly approved or approved. Fewer than one-tenth signified any outright disapproval. Significantly, the apparently least influential group—economic dominants—voiced the most disapproval (20%) or outright ignorance of the Urban League (also 20%).

Nevertheless, the attacks jeopardized the entire financial campaign. Community Chest leaders, who come primarily from the ranks of second-level attributed influentials, responded with a breakfast meeting attended by the staff, the officials, and, as special guests, a moderate number of the top-level attributed influentials of the community. The guests represented some of the major contributors to the Community Chest. Officials wanted and received approval of any future action they might take to defend the continued participation of the Urban League.[5]

After the campaign, a second meeting took place among approximately the same principals. At this session, the Chest officials attempted to gain the group's full approval for continuing the Urban League in the Chest fund. Full agreement on the League's inclusion followed a lengthy discussion. For one year, at any rate, the influentials had vetoed an attempt to change the *status quo* in the private social welfare program of Atlanta. In terms of our scheme, they had given high priority to retention of the Urban League and had legitimatized the value allocation.

The following year, however, three months before the Chest campaign, the states' rights champions once again called for elimination of the Urban League, this time adding to the old charges the new one that the League's financial transactions were not sufficiently audited, that some funds were being passed on to its national headquarters or to those of the National Association for the Advancement of Colored People. Once again, the entire Chest drive was endangered. One solution suggested by the Chest officials was to change the name of the League, but the leaders of the League itself objected to that move. In the meantime, it became clear that the issue had provided a "whipping boy" for Marvin Griffith, outgoing governor of the state, and for W. T. Bodenhamer, the states' rights candidate for governor, who doubled as executive director of the States' Rights Council of Georgia.

Since the Community Chest was committed to the League, it had to arrive at a promotional device that would give its commitment legitimacy in the eyes of the community. In some

desperation, the leading officials and staff personnel began search-
ing for a device that would lend an atmosphere of unimpeach-
able morality to the retention of the League in the drive. One
top professional (a civic staffer) suggested that the giant kickoff
rally, an innovation in itself, feature an address by evangelist
Billy Graham. Although his appearance might have lent the
necessary air of sanctity, the lay leaders of the organization
overruled the suggestion and did not approach Graham. Then
three lay officials, two of whom were attributed influentials,
ingeniously proposed asking Herman Talmadge, the junior
United States senator from Georgia, to speak.

With this agreed-upon strategy, two of them flew to Washington to secure the senator's agreement. An accidental meeting
on the plane with another attributed influential, long reputed
to be one of the most powerful men in Atlanta, enabled the two
intermediaries to strengthen their position. They told him of
the threat to the Chest drive and of their mission to Washington.
He completely supported their strategy, and since he had played
a significant role in helping Talmadge to gain his senatorial
seat, the emissaries presumably were materially encouraged by
his support.

After landing in Washington, they made almost immediate
contact with Talmadge. For one hour and a half, they discussed
with him the problem in Atlanta and how Talmadge could
help alleviate the threat. The senator agreed to address the
kickoff meeting and his speech left little doubt that the Chest
drive had the blessing of a prominent and powerful Georgian
who could in no way be called a liberal in the area of race
relations. Its consequence was to neutralize the attacks of the
ardent states' righters. Also lending political prestige to the
affair was Mayor Hartsfield_a, who is not usually in close agreement with the senator and whose presence added the blessing
of the more liberal socio-political forces in the community. In
this fashion, then, legitimation was accomplished. Implementation was not a key part of this particular decision process.

To employ their veto power effectively in this case, the
actors did, of course, follow a series of steps that could be
designated as attempts at positive power. In terms of the major
question at stake, however, the final action is essentially an
expression of veto power. In sum, the maneuver delivered the

coup de grâce to opponents of the Urban League—and as a final blow, Senator Talmadge refused to address the States' Rights Council during his visit to Atlanta.

"Typical" Decision-Making: An Omnibus Bond Issue

Examples of the decision-making process and dimensions of power have so far not touched on the well planned, elaborated structure typical of much major policy-making in Atlanta. A case study of the Atlanta-Fulton County Joint Bond Issue for approximately $87 million is more representative of the "normal" modes of policy-making, at least when large-scale physical improvements are involved. By most standards, the process of decision-making on this issue cannot be termed controversial, which, of course, does not lessen the importance of the issue or its utility in studying community decision-making.

Projections of future growth and accompanying costs are not unfamiliar in Atlanta. One planning agency, the Metropolitan Planning Commission, has put great emphasis on anticipating the future of the community and in planning accordingly. An early staff director of the Commission, Phil Hammer$_a$, played an instrumental role in steering the Commission's work in this direction. About a year and a half before the bond issue came to a vote, the Commission, then under the staff supervision of Robert Stuart$_p$ and the lay leadership of Robert White$_a$ and with the consultation of Hammer$_a$, published a report on the capital needs of Atlanta, exclusive of schools, for the next five years. The report was a response to the need for such information by local governments and by an outside consultant who was conducting a survey of the financial needs and resources of the city. While the report's $67 million figure for revenue from bond sources was not phrased as a definite recommendation, its importance as a starting point for thinking about a bond issue was clear to influentials in the community.

Another of the Commission's publications urged a master planning program for the Atlanta metropolitan area. On the basis of these prognostications, many staff-level influentials in the community began to consider the problem of financing the improvements and physical developments that would change the face of the metropolitan area. Roy Ulrich$_x$,[6] chief staff

official of the Chamber of Commerce, became especially interested in the subject. He drafted a memo listing, in summary
form, several projects that would, if investigated and developed,
help to implement the master plan. One involved needs for
capital improvement. He circulated this memo to a half-dozen
attributed influentials who were active in the Chamber, and
he subsequently made personal visits to discuss with them the
innovations necessary to keep pace with the growth of the area.
Similar efforts were being undertaken by other influentials in
the community during this formative stage.

The initiation phase of the decision-making process and
some preliminary priority allocation had thus already been
accomplished. Much work still remained on the allocation front,
however. Not only must the anticipated allocation be technically
sound, but it must also bear the imprint of respected backing.

Recognizing that intensive investigation of bond priorities
would facilitate the work of a citizens' committee to be established later (such committees had operated previously in Atlanta, and the presumption among most participants was that
one would emerge this time too), the Chamber undertook a
detailed examination of city needs, in order to establish basic
guidelines for major portions of the omnibus bond issue to be
offered the following year. In addition to relying upon the
Metropolitan Planning Commission's earlier report on capital-
improvement needs in the city, the Chamber's committee also
talked with city department heads and expert consultants on
specific capital-improvement programs.

Before the actual release of the Chamber report, however,
a complicating factor arose, when it became clear that Fulton
County Commissioners Carlyle Fraser$_a$, James Aldredge$_a$, and
Archie Lindsey, were seriously considering a $5-10 million bond
issue, with the largest share to be spent on county schools.
Rather than inundate the city with bond issues, the city initi-
ators sought to persuade the county officials to postpone their
referendum so that a joint bond issue could be presented later.
Ulrich$_x$ of the Chamber and Chamber President Hix Green$_p$
helped to arrange an evening meeting among Mayor Hartsfield$_a$,
the county commissioners, some key department heads in the
city, and several attributed influentials in the Chamber to
achieve agreement on a joint issue. Thanks partly to the arguments of Superintendent Paul West$_a$ and School Board Chair-

man W. L. Robinson_p, the county commissioners insisted on
reserving the part of the contemplated bond issue designated for
schools for an early vote. Since only county residents living outside the city of Atlanta would vote on the county school bond proposal, this compromise was acceptable to the city representatives.

Phil Hammer_a, who had entered private practice after leav-
ing his staff position with the Metropolitan Planning Commission, served as chairman of the Chamber study committee.
Heading up the four major subcommittees (in terms of financial
outlay) were engineer Donald Dutton for aviation, bank vice-
president George Goodwin_a for streets and highways, attorney
Pope McIntire_p for water and sewers, and retailer Robert Regen-
stein_p for schools. Hill Healan_p, a ranking professional in the
Chamber, served as secretary of the committee. The committee's
recommended expenditures totaled about two-thirds the amount
of those in the Metropolitan Planning Commission's earlier
report for five-year needs. The largest reduction was in the
streets and highways program, for which the first report assessed
necessary expenditures at about $40 million, while the second
placed them at about $20 million. To help on the streets and
highways program, the committee suggested that Fulton County
provide for one-half of the $20 million in its portion of the
joint bond program together with another estimated $10 million
for other needs.

Significantly, the initiation and preliminary allocation of
priorities had come almost entirely from the Chamber. One
of the leaders of the bond program made this comment:

> Hartsfield_a definitely dragged his feet all the way until he was
> really pushed into it by the Chamber. The Metropolitan Planning
> Commission's study was definitely not pitched specifically to a bond
> issue, and I think for the very clear reason that Hartsfield_a would have
> disapproved of their doing so. As I said, Hartsfield_a was definitely
> against talking about a bond issue because he saw an election coming
> up, and he did not want to stick his neck out and talk about huge
> public expenditures.
>
> A number of people on the Chamber, including myself, agreed
> that the time had come for the Chamber itself to take the lead in
> pushing for a bond program. The mayor had been asked repeatedly
> to set up a Citizens' Bond Commission for this same purpose, but he
> had refused to do so. . . . The mayor knew what we were doing and
> did not get in our way, but he certainly did not help any. The various

department heads of the city and county all cooperated with us, particularly after we made it clear that we were going to come up with our own estimates if they did not give us theirs . . . .

The press carried on a continuous needling of Hartsfield$_a$ about when the bond issue should be held and the necessity for speedy action. Significant, too, is the fact that at these early stages the very "top" of the presumed decision-making structure (including the mayor$_a$ and other leading government officials) was · not openly involved, although some members were committed:

> The membership of the Chamber committee was composed of little shots, but all of them extremely competent . . . . There is no question about the fact that most of the top leaders in the Chamber were strong for the bond program and had been arguing that the mayor should set up a commission long before we decided to take the responsibility in the Chamber. People like Richard Rich$_a$ and other downtown leaders were the real supporters. However, as I said, the job was tossed across to some of us on the lower level to put together the basic figures.

Although the Chamber's recommendations carried no official weight, city and county officials monitored them closely. For example, Atlanta's airport has been of particular interest to Hartsfield$_a$, an old-time aviator. When he discovered that the recommended amount for airport construction was $4-5 million lower than he wanted, he attempted to have the figure raised. Two days before the report was to be published, he telephoned at least two members of the Chamber committee. He insisted that certain figures they had used had been misinterpreted. The aviation subcommittee was subsequently approached and, in light of the "misinterpretation," changed its recommendation to a higher figure.

With the adoption of the committee's recommendations by the executive board of the Chamber, a further step had been taken in fixing the allocation of values for the upcoming referendum, which had still not been formally announced. Jack Tarver$_a$, a leading executive in Atlanta newspaper enterprises and a member of the executive board of the Chamber, told Ulrich$_x$, that the two newspapers would be willing to offer their facilities for explaining the Chamber's recommendations. Hartsfield$_a$ also was amenable to opening the promotional and informational stage of the bond issue, even though definite amounts and the date of the public vote had not been set. Four days after the formal release of the Chamber's report, the combined Sunday (December 16, 1956) editions of the *Journal* and *Constitution* carried an extensive section on the proposed bond issue and the Chamber's recommendations. On the same day, the newspapers' television station carried a public-service program on which Hartsfield$_a$ and County Commissioner James Aldredge$_a$ appeared. In addition, the *Journal* began a series of articles dealing with each major section of the proposed issue. Actually then, the promotion phase of the decision-making process had already been entered, although much work still remained on the allocation front.

Because of favorable public reactions to the Chamber's report and the urgent request of the county officials for a bond issue, Hartsfield$_a$ finally consented to appoint city representatives to a Citizens' Advisory Committee (CAC). The other two governmental units involved in the contemplated joint program, Fulton County and the Atlanta Board of Education (an autonomous body), were eager to select their members of the Committee. The critical phase of the entire bond program now began. On the basis of past experience, it seemed probable that the recommendations of the CAC would be accepted without question by the three governmental units involved, as long as the committee was impressive, as earlier ones had been. The composition of the committee would therefore be important, not only in terms of competence, but also in terms of stature, respect, and influence in the community at large. Some projects are lost at this stage of transition between staff work and the formulation of concrete plans with real potential for adoption and implementation. Although the staff work was not so extensive, the case on fluoridation already reported is an example of how some projects do not "get off the ground" at this point.

The main actors in the process now shifted. While the prescribed influentials and some lower-echelon attributed influentials had played the major roles in the earlier stages, more attributed influentials, especially top-level ones, now became openly involved. The central figure in the Citizens Committee was Robert MacDougall$_a$, a long-time resident of the city and successful in construction enterprises. Ten years earlier, he had presided as chairman of a joint city-county bond-issue committee. Since then he had served continuously on a citizens' committee charged with administering the funds from that bond program. Before the appointment of the new CAC occurred, Hartsfield$_a$ contacted MacDougall$_a$ because of the latter's past experience, his familiarity with the needs of the city and county departments, and his personal friendship with the mayor. In their discussion, the mechanics of the program came under scrutiny; on the basis of this and other discussions MacDougall$_a$ decided to sound out other influentials.

He held informal sessions with representatives (all first-level attributed influentials) of Coca-Cola, Rich's, Southern Bell, and First National Bank of Atlanta and with several other civic leaders who expressed in various ways concern for the city's development. All these men gave assurances of their support for the general outline of the program as it affected the three units of government. MacDougall$_a$ also called on Tarver$_a$, and they discussed the role of the press. Tarver$_a$ assured MacDougall$_a$ of the support of the two newspapers. After his reconnoitering, MacDougall$_a$ felt certain that enough institutional support existed in the community to achieve acceptance for a large bond issue.

He continued his entrepreneurial activities during the period of selection of the CAC. It had been fairly clear to a few men from the beginning that MacDougall$_a$ would be chairman of the committee. Working with Hartsfield$_a$ and County Commissioner Archie Lindsey, MacDougall$_a$ selected a majority of the fifteen individuals who later constituted the CAC. Six members came from the county, six from the city, and three from the city schools. MacDougall$_a$ made his choices on the basis of individual interest, competence, prestige, and influence. He clearly wanted Frank Neely$_a$, for example, not only because of his presumed power in the community, but also because Neely$_a$ had participated in virtually every major metropolitan project involving streets and highways for the past thirty years. Another example is Fred Turner$_a$, who, although no expert in the field of urban renewal, did have a thorough knowledge of the downtown area and adjoining property, was relatively free from the demands of work, and enjoyed wide respect in the community. Ben Massell$_a$, a man of considerable wealth and quite knowledgeable about building and construction, was a logical choice for the committee because he could lead the sub-committee on public buildings. If MacDougall$_a$ did not personally select each member of the committee, he at least gave his approval to most of them.

Besides MacDougall, Massell, Neely, and Turner, the fifteen-member committee included four other attributed influentials: W. O. DuVall, financial executive; Charles Mathias, labor leader; businessman-politician Everett Millican; and banker L. D. Milton (Negro). Robert Regenstein, a retail merchant and a prescribed influential, was also included. These nine people composed the bulk of the intra-committee influentials. The other six members tended to be representatives of specific geographical or group interests, and they were chosen to ensure the committee's reputation for "balance" and "representativeness." The formal organization of the committee had also been anticipated. As one participant remarked,

MacDougall$_a$ was appointed to this bond group by the mayor and it was pre-arranged that he was to be chairman. Fortunately, he was elected at the first meeting by a unanimous vote. At the first meeting he promptly appointed men as chairmen of the various subcommittees to serve in the field in which they were most interested. He worked very closely with all these chairmen.

Continuity with the past was provided in two different ways. Five of the members—MacDougall$_a$, Neely$_a$, DuVall$_a$, Mathias$_a$, and Millican$_a$—had served on the old bond committee, which had now been disbanded. MacDougall$_a$, DuVall$_a$, and Regenstein$_p$ had also participated in the Chamber study of city bond needs.

Although most of the appointments were based on strategical considerations, at least two committeemen must have felt some surprise at the reasons for their being selected for competence in specific areas. Turner$_a$, for example, knew little about urban renewal at the time of his appointment. One of his first actions after accepting the chairmanship of the sub-committee was to call on Forsythe Gordy$_p$, the executive secretary for the Central Atlanta Association. At that time, Turner$_a$ was beginning his term of office as president of the organization. He and Gordy$_p$ spent half a day on the subject of urban renewal. At the end of the discussion, Turner$_a$ expressed approval of the general outlines of the program. Milton's$_a$ appointment was also a mild surprise. Neither he nor the Negro community at large had sought a position on the committee. Evidently, however, the school board wanted a Negro on the committee, and Milton$_a$, although not previously very active in public school affairs, had the acumen and prestige to warrant nomination.

In retrospect, it appears that the composition of the Citizens Advisory Committee virtually precluded large-scale, organized opposition to the bond program. Still, a recommended program did have to emerge before ratification could occur. A significant factor helping the committee in this respect was the Chamber's study. Almost all members of the committee acknowledged the facilitating influence of the earlier study.[7] Some of the hearings before the CAC repeated essentially the work of the Chamber, since various department heads stated their needs before both groups. Because of the public nature of the CAC, however, lay citizens' groups (governmental and nongovernmental) associated with the departments also appeared. With the Fulton County requests, duplication was reduced since their claims had not been thoroughly reviewed by the Chamber.

Only two or three major deviations from expected allocations were recommended by the CAC. Original estimates suggested that the city and county together authorize about $20 million on the streets and highways program, sharing the burden equally. The final recommendations of the committee totaled more than $26 million, with the county taking about four-fifths of that total. The increments for streets and highways for the most part arose out of the utilization of access among potential beneficiaries of new projects. For example, one of the largest additions was for $1¼ million for street widening in the heart of the Negro community. A professional (civic staffer) with the Urban League had noticed that no projects of direct benefit to the Negro community were included in early drafts of the streets and highways program, although there were some projects that would have benefited parts of the white community almost exclusively.

He drafted his findings and suggestions and sent them to Milton$_a$, who delivered the memorandum to Neely$_a$ and his subcommittee on streets and highways. The positive assets of a large block of Negro voters in the forthcoming bond referendum were presumed by observers to play a part in inducing the committee to make widening streets a major part of the bond program. Other street improvements, some of which had been suggested but not as "musts" in the Chamber study, were also included in the final bond recommendations.

Efforts to induce the county to share a disproportionate burden of payment for the road program were abetted by the county's superior debt position. If the city could persuade the county to carry a large load, then the city could carry out other needed projects. Evidently MacDougall$_a$, Neely$_a$, and Hartsfield$_a$ were instrumental in persuading the county commissioners of the reasonableness of the arrangement.

With the exception of the airport increase, already presaged at the time of the Chamber report, the only other significant changes were various building projects that county officials insisted must be included. Although no public charges were made, many city participants in the bond program felt that these projects represented "pork barrel" for the county. The consensus is that the CAC accepted these pet projects, rather than risk alienating the county officials or the groups associated with the projected building projects. This *quid pro quo,* or "horse-trading" resulted in raising the total figure for the bond program. To the Chamber's original estimate of $70 million ($50 million for the city and a suggested $20 million for Fulton County), the CAC added another $17 million. In its final form the bond program covered eight separate areas—schools, water and sewers, streets and highways, airport, urban renewal, parks, city buildings, and county buildings.

True to earlier predictions, the three governing bodies ratified without exception the recommendations of the Committee. They also accepted the suggested date for the bond referendum. Hartsfield$_a$ and State Senator Charlie Brown of Fulton County had, some thought, endangered the success of the referendum by attempting to schedule it for after the approaching city primary elections. Hartsfield$_a$ argued that the people should know who was going to spend the money raised by the bond issue. After vigorous opposition in the press and presumably on the advice of MacDougall$_a$ and other Committee members, Hartsfield$_a$ yielded and accepted the CAC's recommendations that the bond vote be held before the mayoralty election. The process then moved into the last phase of the promotional campaign (appeal to the public) and to the climax of its legitimation.

The more formal campaign activities were carried out under

five major sponsors. One program was based on the combined efforts of five downtown organizations—the Chamber of Commerce, the Junior Chamber of Commerce, the Central Atlanta Association, the Retail Merchants Association, and the Traffic and Safety Council. The Chamber took the initiative and supplied most of the financial resources. Although the members of the Citizens Committee consented to serve as a steering committee for this campaign, their work appears to have consisted primarily of ratification of staff work already performed.

Most observers and participants in this promotional campaign thought it a rather humdrum affair, partially because their was no effective opposition. As one civic-staff man noted:

The setup of the campaign organization was an orthodox one designed to disseminate information to the general public so that they could vote intelligently on the bond issue. Included were a membership breakfast of the Chamber for discussion of the bond issue projects; a letter to 200 civic organizations urging them to contact all of their members and get them in turn to contact friends and neighbors; letters to members of the Atlanta Chamber and the members of the other four organizations asking them to impress upon their employees the importance of the bond election and urging them to make it possible for them to go to the polls and vote; the Speakers Bureau, Publicity Division; the newspapers, radio, television, printed matter such as window cards, car cards, billboards.

Gordy$_p$, of the Central Atlanta Association, and Ulrich$_x$, Healan$_p$, and other staff people at the Chamber planned and executed much of the technical promotion. Television and radio personnel, especially Pearcy Hearle$_p$, used their initiative to schedule programs featuring MacDougall$_a$, Hartsfield$_a$, and County Commissioner Lindsey. In addition, MacDougall$_a$ and Hartsfield$_a$ made numerous addresses to civic and luncheon clubs throughout the area in the brief five-week campaign period.

A second major source of support, although not specifically organized, came from candidates for city and educational offices in the election scheduled to follow the bond vote. Almost invariably, they supported the bond issue. By coincidence then, expansion of favorable public opinion was served by the increased flow of information and propaganda from the candidates, whose main interests were tangential to the goals of the bond campaign.

Although the five downtown organizations barely recognized its activities, the Atlanta PTA Council also conducted a grass-roots campaign for passage of the bond issue. Under the leadership of Mrs. Warren Alday$_p$, then president, the Council urged full support for the bond issue, even before the final amount had been determined. Like most of the organizations supporting the bond issue, the Council had a special interest (the $16 million reserved for schools). In hopes of enlisting support from other groups of the community, it gave full approval to all projects. The eighty-two local units of the Council in Atlanta exerted efforts, ranging from mild to heavy, with panel discussions being the most common device for eliciting support.

Another promotional campaign was conducted by the Negro Voters League. With A. T. Walden$_a$ at the helm, the League sponsored six mass meetings in the Negro community for endorsement of the bond issue. Speakers included personnel from the League, the Chamber, and the Atlanta Housing Authority. Of particular interest to the Negroes were the urban renewal and the streets and highway provisions. Except for outside speakers and literature received from the downtown organizations, the League operated its own promotional campaign. Walden$_a$ noted, as did most other promotional people, that generating enthusiasm for a bond issue is an almost insurmountable task.

The final major source of pre-election persuasion came from the League of Women Voters. Mrs. Harry Dunstan$_p$, president, directed the League's activities with virtually no co-ordination with the other campaigns. Television, radio, public meetings and letters to members constituted the League's activities.

Since there was little public opposition, strictly promotional activity was not so important as it might have been in other issues. That is one reason for the shift in personnel from the earlier stage. More prescribed influentials, primarily civic-staff personnel, performed the role of gaining public support. If the issue had been more keenly contested, the attributed influentials would probably have been more fully aroused. Then, too, promotional work involving mass appeals to the community is a professional task for which many businessmen and government officials do not have the technical qualifications and interests. Only in speech-making did the attributed influentials contribute significantly in the formal promotional stage.

Formal legitimation of the bond program was provided by a light vote in both the county and the city; only 21% of those eligible voted. All but three precincts reported heavy majorities in favor of all eight items in the bond program. Margins of victory ranged from five to one on city school bonds to slightly less than two to one on some city and county public building improvement bonds.

Implementation of the bond program is, of course, a long process and will not be discussed here. It is worth noting that the CAC had recommended appointment of a lay committee to oversee expenditures for the $26-million streets and highways program. Both city and county officials approved the proposal. Approximately two months after the election, Mayor Hartsfield$_a$ and County Commissioner Frazer$_a$ named a seven-man board of four laymen and three professionals. From the Citizens Advisory Committee, they picked Turner$_a$ and DuVall$_a$. Robert White$_a$ resigned from his chairmanship of the Metropolitan Planning Commission to accept the chairmanship of the new committee. The fourth lay member was S. R. Young$_p$, a leader in county-planning circles. The three professional members were city traffic engineer Karl Bevins$_p$, city construction chief Ray Nixon$_p$, and Fulton County public works director A. T. MacDonald.

If the foregoing account appears bereft of animated controversy, the reason lies in the precise nature of the issue and the way in which it developed. For the most part, it was a managed affair—well planned and well executed. In addition, there was "something for everybody." Opposition from the general public at large was slight—apathy loomed as the most dangerous opponent. Among the significant political actors who might have led opposition—such as the attributed and prescribed influentials—harmony prevailed. According to their statements, all the attributed and prescribed influentials (as well as economic dominants) who voted cast their ballots for all or most of the eight separate proposals.

Our description of the resolution of this issue has consisted primarily of a qualitative account of the major processes and major actors' roles. We have already indicated the political statuses of the main participants. While the techniques we employed to select the elites did not isolate all the primary actors and influentials, they did identify a large majority of them.

(Chapter 8 deals more specifically with this point.) Our qualitative account did not, of course, describe the rate and level of participation for each status-occupant. From questionnaire data we can suggest five major kinds of participation, three of which deal with the two strategic committees.

Table 18 shows that some actors were completely passive

Table 18. Activities of Status-Occupants in the Omnibus Bond Issue

| Activities | ATTRIBUTED INFLUENTIALS | | PRESCRIBED INFLUENTIALS | | ECONOMIC DOMINANTS |
	First Level	Second Level	Government Officials	Civic Staff	
None	30%*	42%	8%	14%	83%
Campaigned	70	58	92	86	17
Appeared before committees	5	9	62	18	0
Contacted committee members	55	38	58	59	17
Served on committees	30	25	12	18	6
Number	(20)	(33)	(24)	(22)	(19)

*Percentages do not total 100% because many actors performed more than one activity.

on this issue. Since a substantial portion of both the first- and second-level attributed influentials were passive, the notion of a generalized reputed elite that settles all issues in the community is again brought into question. The almost total lack of participation by the economic dominants adds further weight to our observation that they are relatively quiescent in community decision-making. On the other hand, the low rate of nonparticipation among prescribed influentials does not necessarily mean that they monopolized the key roles. Except for a few individuals, the intensive campaigning (promotional stage) did not require much work from the actors. As we have already noted, the continual conditioning of the public by previous bond issues and the reinforcement provided by the press made promotional work less important than it would be in more controversial issues.

Appearing before committees, personally making contact with committee members, and serving on committees were more decisive in this decision-making process. Government officials outdistanced other status-holders in committee appearances. Such appearances and the resulting testimony and evidence are classic examples of attempts to exercise filter power. By selectively exposing committee members to information, government officials sought to achieve their own ends. Alone, they did not have the authority to achieve the realization of goals, but through selective exposure of information they could help to influence goal selection and the allocation of values.[8] The hearings also served as propaganda channels for the government officials to create and maintain favorable public opinion. The predominance of government officials over other actors in this role, especially in an issue of this kind, is not surprising. Their success can be measured in part by the huge sum included in the bond program.

Contacting members of a committee is also an attempt at filter power. Such contacts are direct attempts to achieve certain ends or to block other ends. In financial allocation, the tendency is toward positive power acts rather than toward veto acts, especially in an omnibus bond package. Most intercessions by personal contact took the form of petitions for allocations for certain goals, rather than attempts to block other goals. The data (Table 18) demonstrate that, while attributed and civic-staff influentials appeared only infrequently before the committees, they did have many personal contacts with committee members. Their role requirements and expectations did not permit or require public testimony, but they did permit communication by personal contact. That a majority of the government officials also used personal contact attests that the semi-public appearances were often combined with other forms of interaction with committee members.

Finally, serving on one or both of the committees is an example of potential positive and veto power. The committees, especially the CAC, offered this potential because of the semi-authoritative nature of their work. Both the Chamber committee and the CAC had to make decisions reflecting their selection of values to be emphasized for the community. The CAC, for example, pared $13 million from the recommendations of its subcommittees—exercise of veto power. The attributed influentials clearly outranked the other elites in committee assignments (Table 18). With few exceptions, they served on the Citizens Advisory Committee, rather than on the less authoritative Chamber committee. Actually then, although attributed influentials showed less over-all participation in the bond program than did the prescribed influentials, they did dominate the most determinative body in specifying the bond program—the Citizens Advisory Committee. The importance of this differential is underlined by a look at the proportions of all status-holders who served on committees. Of the twenty-two who served on at least one, fourteen were attributed influentials, seven were prescribed influentials, and only one was an economic dominant.

The three issues examined in this chapter have been highlighted in terms of our analytical scheme. Although two cases are certainly not enough to warrant generalization, the examples of veto power indicate the ability of strategically located individuals, both reputed and prescribed influentials, to prevent the attainment of goals that would alter the *status quo*. Other events occurred during the course of our study that substantiate this appraisal, however, including the refusal to establish a biracial committee on race relations and the rejection of a strong home-rule bill for Atlanta.

On the major issue, the omnibus bond proposal, the full panoply of decision-making roles and types of power came to light. Status-holders from the elites, except the economic dominants, were involved at all stages in the decision-making process, an important reminder that roles cut across statuses. Nevertheless, the prescribed influentials and second-level attributed influentials were relatively more active at the initiation and campaigning stages, while the attributed influentials were more active at the allocating and semi-legitimizing stages. To a certain extent, the exercise of positive power and filter power paralleled the roles enacted by the different status-holders. Even though the importance of the bond issue for Atlanta and Fulton County cannot be denied, substantial proportions of each elite participated hardly or not at all. Most of the critical roles in the decision-making process (except for legitimation by the voters) were, however, performed by prescribed or attributed influentials.

NOTES

1. The scheme used in this and the following chapter is drawn from various sources in the literature, as well as from certain specific processes encountered in analyzing the research for the present study. No claim is made for the inherent superiority of this scheme over others. It seemed simply a useful means by which to order and interpret the data for this study. For reference to more detailed guides, see Paul Wasserman, *Decision-*

Making: An Annotated Bibliography (Ithaca: Graduate School of Business and Public Administration, Cornell University, 1958); and Richard Snyder and James Robinson, *National and International Decision-Making*, Program of Research No. 4, Institute for International Order, 1961.

2. All the issues cited could, of course, be subjected to much more intensive examination and reporting. Our purpose is to present the major events and processes of each in terms of the analytical scheme. Newspapers and other printed materials, informal interviews, and data gathered during the structured interviews served as sources of information for these case studies. Because of their special nature, the initial sources of interview information are not cited. In some instances, the actors under discussion are not identified by name.

3. Critics of the issue-approach to studying community power make a similar point: that the approach may well overlook issues of great importance to the community that are kept below the surface of public consideration and decision-making by men of power in the community. Peter Bachrach and Morton S. Baratz advance this argument in "Two Faces of Power," *American Political Science Review*, LVI (December, 1962), 947-52; as does Thomas J. Anton in "Power, Pluralism, and Local Politics," *Administrative Science Quarterly*, 7 (March, 1963), 425-58.

4. Fluoridation appears to be an issue that does, however, lend itself to manipulation by nonbusiness-dominated organizations and government officials. In Raleigh, North Carolina, for example, the Junior League, a women's organization, seems to have played the leading role in a successful attempt at exercising positive power, by having fluoridation installed. Atlanta, though, is not so susceptible to grass-roots movements—the system of checks is too strong to allow any organization like the Junior Chamber of Commerce to win its goal without the collaboration and leadership of more powerful elements in the community. One of the few exceptions to this rule—and a partial one at best—was the movement to keep the public schools open in the face of desegregation in 1961.

5. Another purpose of the meeting was to arrange for commitments of $75,000 from the guests should the organization lack that much of meeting its goal. Since the campaign failed by an even larger margin, this promissory note was not used.

6. Ulrich was about to retire when this study was initiated. He therefore failed to qualify as either a prescribed or attributed influential. Had the research been conducted earlier, however, he would certainly have been classified in one of the two categories. References to him will be accompanied by the subscript X.

7. The close relationship and mutual respect between Hammer, who had directed the Chamber study, and MacDougall also helped to smoothe the transition between the work of the two committees.

8. Students of organization theory will recognize the resemblance of filter power to March and Simon's concept of "uncertainty absorption." As these two writers note, "In a culture where direct contradiction of assertion of fact is not approved, an individualist who is willing to make assertions, particularly about matters that do not contradict the direct perceptions of others, can frequently get these assertions accepted as premises of decision." James S. March and Herbert A. Simon, *Organizations* (New York: John Wiley & Sons, Inc., 1958), p. 166.

7

DECISION-MAKING ROLES

AND TYPES OF POWER:

IN MORE CONTROVERSIAL AND

LESS ROUTINE ISSUES

THE MAJOR ISSUE treated in the previous chapter was a rather noncontroversial matter; the processes and techniques were typical of decision-making on physical improvements in Atlanta.[1] In this chapter, we turn to two issues that were controversial. Both resulted in challenges to the major institutional sources of decision-making in Atlanta. The first issue was a mayoralty campaign and election; the second involved the urban-renewal program, particularly one part of that program.

Mayoralty Election

Mayor William Hartsfield[a] has had a long political career in his home town, Atlanta. Beginning in 1923, he served as alderman for six years and then as a state legislator before his first election as mayor in 1936. Since then, he had been mayor, except for one two-year period, until his retirement in 1961. After a defeat in 1940, he came back to win a special election by an overwhelming majority. Hartsfield's$_a$ support emanated from four main sources: business leaders, who provided financial and strategic aid; most of the city administration and board of aldermen; the middle- and upper-class voting precincts; and, increasingly over the years, the Negro precincts.

Hartsfield$_a$ was the ideal incumbent in a weak mayor system, for he had the temerity and political shrewdness to exercise leadership despite the constraints of the formal governmental structure. His very strengths, however, were also weaknesses that alienated many citizens of Atlanta. The Atlanta newspapers, for example, although they eventually gave him their electoral support, on some occasions aimed caustic shafts at him. Editor and publisher Ralph McGill$_a$ said of him: "because he is of an intense and impulsive nature, he creates many unnecessary foes and often exasperates those who regard him fondly after seeming to go out of his way to make it difficult for those who wish to support him."[2]

In Hartsfield's$_a$ most recent primary fight, in 1957, he barely eked out a victory over his opponent, Fulton County Commissioner Archie Lindsey. Hartsfield's$_a$ dependence on both the upper and lower socio-economic strata was clearly demonstrated by the financial aid and voting support he received. He had relied upon his usual campaign oratory and public addresses to carry him through. The coincidence of the omnibus bond program with the mayoralty primary campaign greatly increased the incumbent's opportunities for exposure and speechmaking. Despite the carping of the press during much of the campaign, the *Constitution* and the *Journal*—and the *Daily World* as well —endorsed him. Still, toward the end of the campaign, he realized that he was in a tough race and that he needed more money to carry out his campaign. A few days before the election, a close friend (an attributed influential) was informed that Hartsfield$_a$ was in need of funds. The friend replied that he would do his best to help.

The benefactor immediately phoned a number of his own associates (a large proportion of whom were attributed influentials) who wanted a continuation of the incumbent administration and the general direction of Atlanta's development. He told them straightforwardly about the request he had received; all indicated their willingness to contribute. About one hour later, the benefactor collected the donations in person and immediately transformed them into cash. He then went directly to Hartsfield's$_a$ office, laid down several thousand dollars in cash, and said, "Here's what you need Bill; it comes from some of your friends around town." Although Hartsfield$_a$ may have known the general source of these funds, he did not know the specific contributors nor the amounts they had given. Specific political obligations and political demands were thus avoided.

In edging out Lindsey, Hartsfield$_a$ followed a long established pattern in his elections. He carried the more prosperous precincts of the city (although voting was lighter than usual there), held his ground spottily in other areas of the city, carried the predominantly Negro districts by heavy majorities, and soundly lost in the lower middle-class and lower-class white sections of the city. Although he had never done well in these last wards, he publicly noted his astonishment at their outright rejection of him. Hartsfield's$_a$ voting support thus came from both the upper and lower (assuming Negro status in the South) socio-economic extremes.

While Hartsfield$_a$ expressed concern with the distribution of his vote, some of his political advisers were privately expressing more sophisticated partisan worries about the pattern. Two of them, both second-level attributed influentials, had frequently supplied the mayor with technical and political information. We shall refer to these two actors as "Alpha$_a$" and "Beta$_a$". They analyzed the returns and recognized that the strong anti-Hartsfield vote represented a distinct threat to the acknowledged coalition that governed the community—the loose alliance between business-civic leaders, Negro leaders, and Hartsfield$_a$ and his administration. It was a very real threat because, according to private surveys recently completed at that time, a substantial proportion of Atlanta's newcomers were from the rural areas of Georgia. In the primary election, more of these people had apparently voted than ever before, and they had expressed their rural attitudes and prejudices by voting against an urbane and moderate mayor. Numerically, Alpha$_a$ and Beta$_a$ reasoned, these immigrants could well shift the balance against the combined Negro and upper middle-class voters who had given Hartsfield$_a$ the primary victory.

Ordinarily such considerations would not have constituted a problem for the mayor and his friends. The winner of the "nonpartisan" primary election is usually elected in light balloting in a general election six months later. Independent candidates can, however, qualify to run against the nominees. Hartsfield$_a$ had once been so challenged by a businessman and had defeated him handily. Less than a month after Hartsfield's$_a$ narrow victory in the 1957 primary, however, speculation abounded that an independent candidate would challenge the mayor, and that other nominees would also be opposed in the election. By the end of the second month after the primary, such a mayoral candidate had emerged. In his opening statement, he declared that he was running because he felt the people wanted a businessman, rather than a politician, at the city's helm. While he had had little previous political experience, other potential candidates with much more political acumen and experience also began to appear.

In the midst of these ominous warnings, Alpha$_a$ and Beta$_a$ and two or three of their associates (one of whom was a civic staffer) communicated to a half-dozen or so key Hartsfield supporters their concern over the primary-vote distribution and its possible meanings in the event of a serious challenge in the general election. Those key supporters included five first-level attributed influentials, three of whom had played significant roles in the bond-issue program and one of whom was among the mayor's closest friends.

On our decision-making continuum, we may call this step the initiation stage. Undoubtedly some of the events that followed would have occurred even if analysts of the primary had not brought the matter to the attention of others with greater power resources at their disposal. But this example of filter power marked the first major step to thwart any attempt to deprive Hartsfield$_a$ of his seeming victory.

The next step consisted of an event apparently unprecedented in Atlanta. Under the guidance of two or three of the alerted group of attributed influentials, a conference of about twenty "top leaders" was held. Some men returned from outside the city to attend the session. Such strategy sessions are usually held among a much smaller group of people or even by phone. In this case, however, a consciously organized and planned meeting was arranged. Apparently, the threat posed by the Citizens

Council's attempt to have the Urban League dropped from the United Appeal (see pp. 111-4) added further urgency to the need for a "summit" meeting. Both the electoral threat to Hartsfield$_a$ and the Community Chest conflict stemmed from the same basic source—discontent among conservative, rural-minded citizens.

Those at the meeting (only one who was invited failed to attend) numbered about twenty. They included approximately fifteen attributed influentials, most of whom had considerable access to financial resources and some of whom themselves held elective or appointive governmental positions. The rest were all financially affluent. Virtually all attending were well known to one another.

The meeting resulted in a firm resolve among the participants that they would strongly support Hartsfield$_a$ both financially and in other ways against any electoral challenge. They did, however, want some guarantee that he would promote and enact a more vigorous and constructive program for the city to replace the current rather opportunistic strategy. Subsequently, two or three members of the "junta" met with Hartsfield$_a$ himself, communicating their all-out support and their suggestions for a more constructive program. Actually these suggestions came from Alpha$_a$ and Beta$_a$, who had been asked by the larger group to prepare a statement of community needs for further development. In a later consultation between the mayor and Beta$_a$, it seemed clear that Hartsfield had taken the advice seriously. Hartsfield$_a$ had prepared an agenda that bore remarkable resemblance to the one Alpha$_a$ and Beta$_a$ had submitted to the top influentials only a short time before.

On our continuum, the conference of influentials represents the priority-fixing stage in the decision-making process of the mayoralty election. The conferees agreed that Hartsfield$_a$ must be re-elected in order for the city to continue its general direction of development. Although they may not have mentioned it openly, their continued high access to the mayor's office constituted another equally strong reason for their defense of the mayor. In exchange for their all-out support, they bargained for the introduction or extension of certain values in the city's development plans.

Once the commitment to Hartsfield$_a$ had been made, most of those at the original meeting retired from active participation. They did, of course, raise funds and communicate with other important actors in the community, but organized planning of campaign strategy with the mayor was limited to a few individuals to whom this task had been delegated at the original meeting. These individuals included three second-level attributed influentials (including Alpha and Beta), one first-level influential who served as informal chairman, two prescribed influentials, and three others. Although Hartsfield$_a$ did not accept all the recommendations and suggestions of this strategy group, his later campaign was affected in the direction of the group's proposals.

This arrangement is one aspect of utilizing resources for gaining acceptance of the chosen alternative. In addition to advising Hartsfield$_a$ on strategy, the group also persuaded press executives to be more gentle and positive in their treatment of him. A survey of the two major papers reveals, in fact, that, after the initial threat to his apparent victory and recognition of the potential anti-Hartsfield$_a$ vote, they did indeed change their approach to the mayor and his administration.

Meanwhile the potential opposition gathered momentum. A newly formed Atlanta Improvement Association decided to hold a nominating convention. Since the Atlanta primary had been conducted without partly labels, this group argued that the winners were not official Democratic nominees. The Association planned to nominate a candidate to run against Hartsfield$_a$ and did not preclude the possibility of nominating candidates for aldermen as well. Another group—closely allied with the Association—was directed by an unsuccessful candidate for city board of aldermen. This movement sought petition signatures and other forms of support for a two-time loser to Hartsfield$_a$. Lines of communication between the two groups were close.

Both Hartsfield$_a$ and Margaret MacDougall$_p$, chairman of the city's executive committee in charge of elections, denounced the proposed convention and plans to place people on the ballot via the petition route as unfaithful to the purpose of the primary. The Improvement Association received another setback from Governor Marvin Griffith, who declined an invitation to address one of their meetings.

The self-styled "Democrats" of the city held their convention, attended by a handful of people. They did not nominate candidates at that convention. Subsequently, however, they sent "Democratic pledge cards" to the winners of the primary asking for their allegiance to the party. Former State Senator Everett Millican$_a$, informed of the letters and pledge cards, advised each nominee by special delivery letter that he had been "chosen as a nominee in a perfectly legal and regular primary . . . which has always been recognized as a regular Democratic Primary." He urged them not to sign the cards. His advice was followed.

As the deadline for qualification drew near, the mayor's twice-defeated opponent withdrew. But restaurateur Lester Maddox, a political neophyte, gathered sufficient signatures on petitions to qualify as an opponent. The disgruntled "Democrats" of the city failed to name a slate after two abortive public meetings. In fact, they eventually voted to support all the primary nominees. The Improvement Association was also disbanded, although Maddox undoubtedly gained support from its former membership.

In the ensuing campaign, Maddox emphasized the mayor's moderate stand on racial matters, hit at his dictatorial administration, and spoke of corruption. Hartsfield$_a$ concentrated on the more positive aspects of his program and often avoided the temptation to argue the race question. The general election brought a turnout only slightly below that of the primary. Hartsfield$_a$ scored a decisive two-to-one victory over Maddox. True to expectations, the victor carried the higher socio-economic precincts and the Negro precincts to achieve his margin. This election marked the legitimation phase.

We may look upon the contest as a struggle between episodic and permanent political influentials. Neither Maddox nor most of his leading supporters had played a significant part in past decision-making in Atlanta. Conversely, Hartsfield$_a$ and his major supporters had not only been seriously involved in other elections but had also exercised influence in a wide range of other policy-making processes in the city. Over the years, various anti-Hartsfield elements in the city had opposed him in one way or another. In this particular election, the principal opponents offer especially good examples of sporadic participants. Although they did not achieve their ultimate goal of winning the mayor's office, they did continue the open opposition to the mayor and to those parts of the power structure associated with him. Maddox, however, later emerged as the main opponent to Ivan Allen, Jr.$_a$, Hartsfield's successor, in the 1961 election. In the following year, he gained a run-off election for the office of lieutenant governor but was defeated.

The successful engineering of Hartsfield's$_a$ victory may also be viewed as an example of the successful exercise of positive power. The individuals who supported the mayor (including himself) were able to achieve their goals completely. No visible concessions were granted the opposition.

We have so far stressed the most important actors in this issue. We noted that both prescribed and attributed influentials, especially the latter, played leading roles. Turning to the questionnaire data, we can outline more generally the relative participation of the status-groups in the issue. As Table 19 shows,

Table 19. Activities of Status-Occupants in the Mayoralty Campaign

Activities	ATTRIBUTED INFLUENTIALS		PRESCRIBED INFLUENTIALS		ECONOMIC DOMINANTS
	First Level	Second Level	Government Officials	Civic Staff	
None	5%*	9%	21%	14%	5%
Spoke to friends	75	91	75	73	95
Urged members of organizations to vote	65	58	33	59	42
Contributed money	55	48	29	18	40
Helped devise campaign strategy	50	27	21	18	0
Helped formulate platform	35	27	21	14	5
Gave public endorsement	30	21	7	23	21
Did publicity work	35	21	17	27	5
Number	(20)	(33)	(24)	(22)	(19)

*Percentages do not total 100% because most actors performed more than one of the activities.

the attributed and prescribed influentials outrank the economic dominants in virtually all the more critical types of electoral participation. This preponderance is especially clear in such categories as developing campaign strategy, helping formulate the platform, and handling publicity. The attributed influentials tend to be slightly more engaged in the crucial activities than do the prescribed influentials. This engagement is partly the result of reluctance among some professional government officials, particularly those working for Fulton County, to become active in political campaigns.

That no more than 65% of the first-level and 58% of the

second-level attributed influentials performed any of the actions listed (with the exception of speaking to friends) is strong evidence against presuming a very extensive general elite that can be defined on the basis of nomination-attribution. Attributed influentials do contribute the largest share of individuals performing critical roles. Although they compose only 47% of our total sample of status-occupants, they account for 54% of those engaging in publicity activities, 59% of the financial contributors, 64% of the platform builders, and 68% of the strategy planners.[3]

We noted at an earlier point that Hartsfield's$_a$ success in holding office for an extended period of time derived in part from the financial and strategic support of leading business interests in the community. Approximately two years after the general election of 1957, it became apparent that this business leadership might withdraw its support from Hartsfield$_a$. Several factors accounted for the change of attitudes. Hartsfield$_a$ was growing old, and his cantankerous behavior seemed to be increasing. He had fought a series of political contests that had gradually created considerable hostility among voters in the city. Finally, he seemed to be losing control over the aldermen's board. (The next issue with which we shall deal provides the most graphic example of his weakened position.) Aldermen did not identify with him so strongly as they had before. Newer political figures were coming onto the scene, and many of them did not feel so indebted to him and his coalition as had others in the past.

There were at least one formal and two informal clues that Hartsfield's tenure might be ending. The first involved a first-level attributed influential, a man probably as close to the mayor as any top influential in the city, who had suffered from the mayor's waning control over the aldermen's board. He reported that, at one of his not infrequent dinners with the mayor, he had indicated that he and other of the mayor's friends thought that Hartsfield$_a$ should probably not run for office again. "Then," he said, "I suggested that Hartsfield$_a$ indicate his preferences for the next mayor and that we would try to go by his recommendations. The mayor is a good politician; he knows who could be elected and he knows who would make a good mayor." Unless radical events intervened, it seemed highly probable that Hartsfield$_a$ would heed this advice.

A second informal move came when Hamilton Douglas$_a$

resigned from the city board. Everett Millican$_a$ was selected by the mayor and the board to replace him. Part of the early strategy in placing Millican$_a$ on the board was the possibility of grooming him for the mayor's seat. Millican$_a$ was amenable to such a move.

A more formal notice of all-out opposition to Hartsfield$_a$ was the announcement of three candidacies for the mayoralty. Included among these candidates was James Aldredge$_a$ from the county commission.

The final decision on whether Hartsfield$_a$ would run again perhaps hinged on the advice of Robert Woodruff$_a$ of Coca-Cola. It is no secret that Woodruff$_a$ had supported Hartsfield$_a$ in the past and that there is mutual respect between them. As one informant remarked:

There is probably only one business interest that Hartsfield$_a$ would not buck if he *really* wanted something. And that is the Coca-Cola outfit. There is a tacit understanding that if Hartsfield$_a$ cannot raise enough money elsewhere then Woodruff$_a$ will ultimately furnish it to him. Let me give you an example of how the mayor is tied to Woodruff$_a$.

Not long after I first acquired my governmental position I and some of my colleagues had before us a measure which would have involved regulating some of the advertising practices of Coca-Cola. Let's call that Item A. We also had another measure which we will just call Item B. Well, one day the mayor called us into his office on the pretext of discussing Item B.

When we walked in there was the mayor and three representatives from Coca-Cola, including the major hatchetman, _____$_a$. After the introductions were concluded, _____$_a$ started talking about Item A, not Item B. He would talk a while, then ask us if we didn't agree with him. Frankly, most of us didn't, and we said so. Then he would go on, all the time becoming more excited.

Finally Hartsfield$_a$ intervened with words something like these: "Now boys, Coca-Cola is a friend of the city and has done a lot for the city. I'm sure we wouldn't want to do anything to hurt them." Well, when he said that we had no real recourse. The motion was made, seconded, and carried that Item A be constructed so as not to hurt the company. I've seen Woodruff's$_a$ hand in matters subsequent to this. The mayor responds to him.[4]

Postscript. As it developed, Hartsfield$_a$ did decide against running for re-election in 1961, probably for many reasons. As a successor, he first seemed to favor M. M. ("Muggsy") Smith$_a$, a state representative from Fulton County. Smith$_a$ was also the choice of the younger and more forceful Negro leaders. Much of the big-business community, however, rallied to the support of Ivan Allen, Jr.$_a$, a well-to-do merchant from an established Atlanta family. Banker Mills B. Lane, Jr.$_a$, is said to have led the fight for Allen$_a$, and he eventually persuaded much of the Hartsfield$_a$ clique to back Allen$_a$. The other serious candidates were Fulton County Commissioner James H. Aldredge$_a$ and Lester Maddox, the unsuccessful challenger to Hartsfield$_a$ in 1957. Allen$_a$ and Aldredge$_a$ adopted a moderate position on the race issue. Allen$_a$ and Maddox emerged as the two top vote-getters in the primary. In the run-off election, Allen$_a$ defeated Maddox by a sizable margin. Allen$_a$ relied on much the same voting coalition as had Hartsfield: the Negro and the higher socio-economic-class white precincts.

Urban Renewal and Public Housing

Atlanta has been late in adopting urban-renewal and re-development programs of the post-World War II type. Part of the difficulty lay in state laws that prohibited resale to private enterprise of land purchased by the government. Even when the laws were changed, the city administration took no strong steps to enact an urban-renewal program. Coupled with the lack of cohesion among business interests in the city and especially among the real-estate companies, this diffidence produced a slow-moving program.

By the time the 1957 omnibus bond program described in the previous chapter came to be formulated, the city finally stood ready to ask the voters for a sizable sum to match federal aid for an urban-renewal program. Among the key influentials at this initiation stage were Hartsfield$_a$ and city officials Wyont Bean$_p$, M. B. Satterfield$_p$, Malcolm Jones$_p$—and Hamilton Douglas$_a$, who served on the board of aldermen.

Although both the Metropolitan Planning Commission and the Chamber of Commerce recommended $1 million for the urban-renewal portion of the bond issue, the planning and housing officials urged the Citizens Advisory Committee to increase that figure to $3 million. The subcommittee, headed by

Fred Turner$_a$, did indeed recommend the latter figure. The full committee cut the request by half, which still left $.5 million more than the earlier figure. After this allocation phase, the urban-renewal portion of the entire bond program underwent the general promotion and legitimation outlined in the preceding chapter. The urban-renewal issue passed by a margin of two to one, one of the smallest margins in the omnibus proposal.

Two important subsequent efforts were designed to accelerate and *implement* the urban-renewal program, which still lagged, despite the public's expressed approval. Alderman Douglas$_a$ sponsored the creation of an urban-renewal department for the city. He argued that the new department was necessary "because urban renewal has grown into a complicated process." The board of aldermen fully approved establishment of the new department. Hartsfield$_a$ appointed Malcolm Jones$_p$ its first director. In addition to working on slum clearance and redevelopment, Jones$_p$ proved a vigorous prosecutor of the toughened city housing code, a vital part of the urban-renewal program.

The second effort was designed to encourage lagging citizen enthusiasm. Nearly two and one-half years after the board of aldermen had given authorization, Hartsfield$_a$ appointed a Citizens' Advisory Committee for Urban Renewal. Instead of a large body, as he had originally suggested, he named a nine-man committee "to guide, influence and prepare citizen acceptance of Urban Renewal." Cecil Alexander$_p$, an architect prominent in local and state architectural organizations, was appointed chairman. The only member of the committee from the first level of the perceived influentials was Ivan Allen, Jr.$_a$, who was later elected mayor.

Alexander$_p$ labored with his small committee for over a year. Soon both he and urban-renewal director Jones$_p$ realized that, to achieve acceptance of a continuing urban-renewal program in the community, they needed a citizens' committee representative of more key institutions in the city. As one participant said, "We needed some big names on the committee, people with prestige as well as influence. Our small committee just didn't have enough of either." Working with Hartsfield$_a$, Alexander$_p$ and Jones$_p$ helped to select an eighty-seven-man committee, which included a significant number of the presumed leadership of the community. Seven of the thirteen members on its executive committee were attributed influentials, and most of the others represented recognizable sources of institutional strength. Nine of the thirteen members on the Land Development Committee, a subcommittee of the larger group, were attributed influentials. Negroes composed one-third of the membership of the full committee. This enlargement of the citizens' committee is a striking demonstration of how and why prescribed influentials need and "use" attributed influentials to achieve desired goals. In view of the strong action many of the appointees later took in defense of a broad urban-renewal program, it is also a good example of the unanticipated consequences of such co-optation. As one participant described it, the expansion of the committee occurred in this way:

> Alexander$_p$ and Jones$_p$ suggested at many meetings that we press the Mayor for a larger and more powerful committee. Frankly, I thought it would be impossible to achieve for several reasons: the Mayor's known antipathy to urban renewal at that time, his feeling that leaders in the city would not lend their names or influence to urban renewal, and, most important, his oft-expressed conviction that none of the top-ranking white citizens would serve on a biracial committee.
>
> Alexander$_p$ and Jones$_p$ suggested that, if the Mayor would allow them to use his name, they would undertake to recruit additional committee members by mail. I was positive that no committee could be formed without the personal intervention of the Mayor and that their efforts would be wasted. My reasons were sound, but I had badly misjudged the temper of the leaders on the question of urban renewal. The Mayor, seeing the picture from the other side of the fence, misjudged it as badly as I. Alexander$_p$ and Jones$_p$ are two of the most persistent people I know. They simply badgered the Mayor until he, believing they would fail anyway, agreed to let them mail invitations over his signature to any people they wished.
>
> The results were truly fantastic. There was only one refusal from a list which included virtually every member of the "power structure." . . . From having a "nothing committee," Alexander$_p$ suddenly found himself with a remarkably powerful weapon, which he used to the great advancement of urban renewal in Atlanta.[5]

Alexander$_p$ and others felt that the program profited from the expansion of the committee. On the other hand, Alexander$_p$ suffered limitations on his work because of his lack of high social status in the community. Commenting on his search for a replacement as chairman (a position Alexander$_p$ kept as long

as he did partly out of friendship and obligation to Douglas$_a$),
one participant made the following observation:

This position needs someone who can pick up the phone and talk to
the big boys on a first-name basis. I think Alexander$_p$ really suffered
from a lack of acquaintance and friendship with some of them. They
react and respond to each other. He's contacted a few people about
taking the chairmanship. Some who shouldn't have it want it. Others
who should take it won't have it.

Most of the reputed and prescribed influentials in Atlanta
seemed to approve of Alexander's conduct of his office, although
some thought he used himself too much. They also recognized,
however, that his power potential was curtailed by his lack of
high social and economic status.

Even though Atlanta had the legal authority to proceed
with the urban-renewal program, lack of compliance and acceptance by the general public and specialized publics hampered
for a long time its full implementation, the final stage on our
decision-making continuum. The complete exercise of positive
power was a difficult task. One of the biggest problems, for
example, was relocating those displaced by slum-clearance projects. Only after overcoming the considerable obstruction presented by the "ward courtesy" practice of the aldermanic board
were Douglas$_a$ and others able to designate sites for housing
under Title 221 of the National Housing Act. Although Atlanta
went on to initiate a number of "221" housing starts, by mid-
1959 there still were not enough units to house the expected
displaced group, the majority of whom were Negroes. The
board of aldermen, again under the prodding of Douglas$_a$ and
others, therefore authorized the Atlanta Housing Authority, as
agent for the urban-renewal program, to find sites for 1000 more
units. Because it combines urban renewal and public housing,
because of its controversial and important nature, and because
of its suitability as an example of complex decision-making in
Atlanta, we shall examine this last problem in detail. For analytical purposes, we shall view the ensuing events in terms of the
decision-making continuum we have outlined. The aldermanic
board's action represents the initial stage.

Acting upon the request of the aldermen's board, the Atlanta Housing Authority set about locating sites for the new

low-rent housing. John O. Chiles$_a$, chairman, and M. B. Satter-field$_p$, executive director, were the key Authority officials involved in the selection process. One of the first sites they chose and purchased (known popularly as the Egleston site) cost approximately $.5 million. It was situated in a Negro residential area with a moderate amount of white commercial and industrial activity. Three hundred fifty units were planned for the site. Before the site could be approved by the board of aldermen, it had to be rezoned from industrial to residential usage. The Atlanta-Fulton County Joint Planning Board, with the urging of planner Wyont Bean$_p$ and the backing of Chairman S. R. Young$_p$, unanimously recommended the rezoning.

The proposal then went to the zoning committee of the board of aldermen for preliminary recommendation before final action by the full board. Housing and urban-renewal supporters expected that their initiatory and priority-setting efforts would be successfully carried through to enactment. Neighborhood opposition developed quickly but quietly, however. The ostensible reason for antagonism was the unsuitability of the area for residential use. The claim that residential and business values would decline was also made. These were the manifest objections but intermingled with them were latent factors of racial and class prejudice.

In terms of our paradigm, the opposition forces favored a different ranking of community priorities and values than did the proponents of the site. Leader of the antagonists was Louis Newton, minister of a large Baptist church and chairman of the Georgia Baptist Hospital Commission. A large Baptist hospital is located in the area. A number of neighborhood civic, business, and school organizations also opposed the rezoning. These groups made their views known through the well attended public hearing of the board's zoning committee. They had also made prior contacts with some of the members of the four-man committee. Since chairman Milton Farris$_p$ was out of the city, it was only Mayor Hartsfield's$_a$ vote as an ex-officio member that resulted in a tie vote on the rezoning bid, rather than in defeat.

Urban-renewal and public-housing officials expressed surprise and shock at the committee's close vote. Final action, however, awaited the full board's deliberations. Although Alderman Farris$_p$ supposedly had an agreement that action on this

site would be postponed until a companion site, on which 650
units would be built, could be considered, the opposition forces
on the board forced Farris$_p$ to bring up the Egleston proposal.
The board then voted overwhelmingly (eleven to three, with
two members absent) to reject the rezoning application. The
opposition had successfully exercised veto power. Almost half
the board's voting members had made a prior commitment to
Newton and his church colleagues to disapprove rezoning. Newton had utilized the most potent force at hand to secure his end
—the promises of five or six aldermen. Combined with the votes
of the aldermen who favored ward courtesy over other decisional
premises (the aldermen in the affected ward opposed rezoning)
the opponents scored a decisive victory.

The reaction among the urban-renewal and public-housing
proponents to this stunning defeat was vociferous and characterized by dire predictions about the entire urban-renewal program. Since the proposed 1000 public-housing units were part
of the agreement between the city and the federal government,
rejection would, they said, be fatal to the program unless another
suitable site could be secured. Alexander$_p$, Hartsfield$_a$, Douglas$_a$,
Jones$_p$, and Chiles$_a$ all voiced public disappointment and despair.

Not until this stage did the proponents rally and seek actively to promote their cause. The promotion phase, then, occurred after an initial setback. Alexander$_p$ called a special
meeting of the citizens' committee to consider future action and
to relay the keen disappointment expressed by Negro influentials. Representatives from several downtown organizations, including the Chamber of Commerce and the Home Builders
Association, attended the meeting. A strong commitment to
have the zoning decision reversed emerged from the meeting.

Another meeting, held at the Capital City Club, brought
together urban-renewal and housing officials for a session with
the aldermanic board to reconsider the rejected site. Although
four of the aldermen who had voted against the proposal did
not appear at the session, the meeting did attract one opposition
alderman—Douglas Wood—who stated that he felt a mistake
had conceivably been made and that he was in favor of
reconsideration.

Despite Douglas's$_a$ warning that the time was not propitious
for reopening the case, Wood a short time later did reintroduce
the topic. He submitted it as an ordinance, rather than as a

private petition, thus evading a nominal prohibition against reintroduction of petitions within a one-year time period. In a close vote, the board agreed to reconsider. The cycle then began anew with the Joint Planning Board, which once again voted unanimously for rezoning. But Chairman Young, prophesied correctly, noting that the petition had to receive a public hearing before the zoning committee: "That's where the trouble may come. They are politicians you know."

The lines were now firmly drawn. For some regular activists in community affairs, alignment came only after readjustment of their value priorities. Conservative businessmen, for instance, had to choose between long-standing antipathy to public housing and urban renewal, on one hand, and their desire for a progressive community, identification with leading businessmen among the proponents, and fear of antagonizing the Negro community, on the other.

Policy-making on this issue thus entered its full-blown promotional stage. Since the proponents knew that they already had sufficient votes to win the committee battle, they immediately directed their efforts to members of the full aldermanic board who opposed the rezoning. This campaigning activity was concentrated on at least three major fronts. One was the persistent pressure of the press, both white and Negro. Cartoons, editorials, and news stories continually reminded citizens and aldermen alike of the import of the vote; that a $20-million-plus urban-renewal program perhaps hung in the balance, that racial tensions in all probability would increase if rezoning failed, that the dislocated had to have some place to live. The mass media thus exerted great efforts for the petition.

Other support came from organized groups in the community. Under pressure from members who were either on the Urban Renewal Committee or were otherwise connected with the urban-renewal program, a wide variety of interest groups came to the support of the site, including the Chamber of Commerce—undoubtedly the single most influential interest group in the community. In order to maintain its cohesion and its essentially conservative nature, the Chamber seldom takes public stands on the very controversial issues in the community. The organization found itself among strange bedfellows—AFL-CIO Council, Urban League, Empire Real Estate Board (Negro), League of Women Voters, United Church Women, National

Association of Social Workers, Atlanta Association for Mental Health, Georgia Engineering Society, Women's Chamber of Commerce, and various others. For such a controversial issue, the alliance was indeed a strange one in its inclusion of civic-business, good government-civic, and civic-welfare organizations. Completing the alliance, in much the same way as in political battles described in legislative studies at the national and state levels, were government officials: the Housing Authority, the Citizens Committee, the mayor, and some of the aldermen.

The efforts of the press and the organized groups were primarily public and indirect in nature. Aldermen assessed their weight in much the same fashion as congressmen appraise the press and group interests on a controversial bill. More direct and less public efforts were also made, however. One small group of men had been holding fairly regular sessions since the early stages of the urban-renewal program. They included, at one time or another, the eight or nine attributed and prescribed influentials who had been most active on this issue from the beginning. During this period, they discussed ways to persuade recalcitrant aldermen to change their votes, as well as more public aspects of strategy. Rather than talk to the aldermen directly, their strategy usually dictated using the interpersonal influence of others close to the aldermen.

Another small group, operating on a more *ad hoc* basis, began to meet after the resuscitation of the rezoning petition. This group—about a dozen at full strength—met for a series of weekly breakfasts, usually in the dining room of a downtown bank. About half the invited guests were also members of the first group. The other half consisted primarily of top-level attributed influentials. Everybody attended at least twice, and some were present for all the sessions. The participants would review the week's happenings, discuss strategy for persuading dissident aldermen, and calculate their prospects for success. Their tactics included direct approaches to aldermen and indirect approaches through such others as aldermen's bankers, personal friends, occupational associates, ministers, and so forth.

One remarkable feature of this campaign lay in the unusual way in which the attributed and prescribed influentials worked in concert. The informal committees provided a graphic demonstration of this heterogeneity. Then, too, the open involvement and public stands of the attributed influentials on such a controversial subject tended to bring the two influential types into closer interaction. Undoubtedly the circumstances and formal procedures involved in this issue served to make the promotional stage extremely important—quite the opposite from its importance for the bond program. Activity that is often the domain of the prescribed influentials and a very few attributed influentials now became the responsibility of others as well. The need for interpersonal influence, in addition to mass influence, helped to make this promotional stage crucial.

By the time the aldermanic committee was ready to hold its public hearing, it was apparent that much more than a relocation site, an urban-renewal program, or racial harmony was involved. The issue had become a tremendously strong test of the generally recognized major sectors of the power structure. The alliance included Hartsfield$_a$[6] and some of his supporters in the city bureaucracy, the respected and influential business organizations, the good-government forces, the almost solid phalanx of Negro leaders and organizations, the highly respectable Citizens Committee, and the press. And this same combination (plus or minus a few elements) had easily prevailed on the bond program, in the 1957 mayoralty election, and in defeating the attempt to oust the Urban League from the Community Chest drive. If now an even stronger alliance failed, it could be a sign of general deterioration of the prevailing power structure.

To be sure, complete cohesion did not exist among all the components. Alexander$_p$, for example, found two or three of his committee members in opposition to him. Some members of the Chamber who had commercial establishments in the Egleston area opposed rezoning. The religious institutions were divided. Finally, the neighborhood civic and businessmen's groups, which usually follow in the wake of the Chamber and the other major organizations, this time deviated from the pattern. Nevertheless, the complex of institutional forces favoring rezoning represented a potent constellation.

While these forces combined, the antagonists attempted to consolidate their position. To the original forces of opposition had been added the antagonism of those in the area of the proposed 650 units (known as the Field Road site); this location was to be considered in the same hearing with the more controversial Egleston site. Although stiff opposition to the newer site arose, it failed to match the intensity associated with the earlier one. A development in opposition strategy was the employment of A. C. ("Pete") Latimer$_a$ as its paid attorney. Latimer$_a$, who was president of the Atlanta Board of Education at the time, gave the opposition a potent new weapon because of his status in the community and the fact that he had, during the most recent city election, won a hotly contested battle against a long-time incumbent. His affiliation with the school board, however, almost hurt his allies, for they were accused of using the schools in the disputed sites as propaganda mills. Latimer$_a$ was also confronted with a conflict-of-interest charge. Despite the uproar, he continued to represent the opposition.

More than 1000 people, an unprecedented number, attended the aldermanic committee hearing. Since the full aldermen's session would not be open for public discussion, the committee meetings provided the one public opportunity for appraisal of the strengths of the competing forces. After an emotional four hours, the committee (with Hartsfield voting) cast a four-to-one vote in favor of rezoning. One remarkable feature of the hearing was the presence and testimony of men who quite often avoid controversial public statements. Richard Rich$_a$ and C. H. Jagels$_a$, for example, represent competing department stores and might not be expected to be overly co-operative with each other. Both testified to demonstrate the unanimity of the "downtown" point of view.

But the full board had still to vote. From the original eleven-to-three tally, the proponents had added the votes of the two favorable aldermen who had been absent at the time of the original vote. In addition the two aldermen who had spearheaded reconsideration of the petition seemed certain supporters. The lineup was then nine to seven, with the president of the board not voting. Two or three more votes were needed for acceptance. Shortly before the meeting (which came two weeks after the committee hearings), proponents predicted a narrow margin of victory. This prognostication rested on three premises: that one of the opposition members (James Jackson), who was recuperating from an operation, would not attend; assurance by a former antagonist on the day preceding the vote that he would vote affirmatively; and the strategy of putting the less controversial Field Road site first on the agenda, where at least one alderman from the Egleston area ward was expected to vote for rezoning, which would in turn cause at least one alderman from the Field Road ward to retaliate by voting for rezoning of the Egleston site.

When the actual vote was cast on March 7, 1960, the Field Road location passed easily, eleven to five. Then came the Egleston vote, and the proponents' premises proved unsound: the recuperating member dramatically entered the chamber and voted against rezoning; the guaranteed defector voted as he had originally; and the whipsaw attempt failed, since no alderman retaliated against one who had voted for rezoning in his own ward. With sixteen voting, the vote was evenly split. Lee Evans$_p$, president of the board, then cast the tie-breaking vote against rezoning. Harstfield$_a$ had predicted before the session that Evans$_p$ would have to break a tie, and Evans$_p$ had evidently anticipated his role, for he had a prepared statement ready at the meeting.

This vote marked the second failure to rezone the Egleston site. Although some Negro leaders and groups called for further reconsideration, the site seemed certain not to become a location for public housing. Actually, the urban-renewal and housing forces had scored a major victory in one sense, for the board had approved the 650-unit Field Road site. Indeed, some people maintain that the "power alliance" prevailed. But a veto had been applied to the controversial site by the antagonists. The proponents failed to exercise complete positive power, even though construction of about two-thirds of the 1000 necessary units was now assured. The alliance reacted keenly to the setback—the first serious one it had suffered in several years.

Many influentials and observers searched for an explanation. One newspaper reporter wrote that "the mayor thought he had the battle in his pocket and was just plain outmaneuvered. He admits it." A civic professional explained:

It's one thing to plan a project from the start and carry it through. It's quite another to jump into it at a later point. No "power structure" anywhere can jump into battle at the halfway point and come out on top. Too much had been done by the opposition beforehand; they had too many aldermen committed. You can't expect the "power structure" to perform miracles.

Evidently, too, the "power structure" had failed in its monitoring function. As one attributed influential put it, "The power structure did not have its antennae out. This whole thing slipped up on us." Yet the defeat seemed the result of more than merely bad strategy or poor monitoring. Wrote one newsman:

As to the question of what happened to the mayor's influence—the vote served well to explain the phrases applied to Atlanta's form of government, a weak mayor system, to which is generally added, "with a strong mayor."

Obviously, the latter part of the term applied more properly on some issues than others. In this instance several of the mayor's strongest backers voted against the rezoning while some of those who opposed him supported it.

Other observers directed attention to the coalition of which Hartsfield$_a$ was a part:

Hartsfield and his colleagues are getting old; he has absorbed few new people into his orbit. Some of the younger people, such as Latimer, do not feel committed to the mayor and the group around him.

Another commented:

For years the business side of the power structure has relied on Hartsfield to keep the board in line. They would back him and not pay too much attention to the aldermen because they were in with him. Now that Hartsfield's control is slipping we are going to have to start watching the aldermen more closely. This includes getting them elected.

To appreciate the extent of the possible restructuring of decision-making, of which this issue was a portent, it is necessary to realize that Latimer$_a$, the lawyer for the opposition, had run as a "reform" school-board candidate with the quiet support of some of the business elements that were later deeply committed to rezoning the controversial site. One man involved in the urban renewal-public housing controversy revealed that:

I ran into Latimer when all this was going on. I told him, "I put up . . . so that you could run for your office. Now, I don't mind your questioning my judgment, which you have done in opposing me this way. But I do mind your questioning my motivations and intent, which you have done by your accusations and insinuations."

Yes, we're going to make some people remember how they voted and acted on this matter.

If the white influentials were upset by the outcome, the Negro leaders were more disturbed and even vindictive. One leading Negro political figure said:

We have a list. We know how everybody voted on the crucial votes. Even though the next election is over a year away we won't forget. That includes Latimer.

Another noted at a meeting called by some Negro leaders:

We've been voting for Lee Evans practically in a bloc since 1939, and now look what he did. I've voted for him for the last time.

Perhaps the alliance's ability to preserve itself in power or to co-opt new elements of governmental leadership will determine whether or not the configuration of power remains substantially the same or is radically altered. The peaceful desegregation of schools in 1961 and the election of another moderate as mayor suggested that the coalition was still intact.

Summary

The two cases discussed in this chapter illustrate roles and types of power in resolving controversial issues. In the mayoralty election, there was virtually unanimous agreement among the actors as to their ranking of preferences—Mayor Hartsfield was first. Controversy occurred only in other parts of the community. On the urban renewal-public housing issue, unanimity was not so complete, nor were the preferences of equal intensities—that is, some opposition did develop in the ranks of the actors under study, and, even among those who favored the proposal, some were rather mild in their enthusiasm. But, as in the first case, there was also stout opposition from other segments of the community.

In the mayoralty campaign, the attributed influentials were particularly significant at the initiating and priority-fixing stages. The promotional stage brought the further involvement of the prescribed influentials although some attributed influentials continued to be active. Since legitimation occurred in the public vote, the voting behavior of the status-holders is of negligible importance, except as it reflects their commitment to working for Hartsfield's$_a$ election. The entire issue was a demonstration of the successful exercise of positive power. A good example of filter power occurred when a small group of civic staffers and second-level attributed influentials warned of the lurking danger in the distribution of the mayor's support and recommended a program of action. An unprecedented caucus of the self-designated "leaders" of Atlanta (primarily first-level attributed influentials) highlighted the conscious attempt to achieve desired goals.

In the second issue, urban renewal-public housing, the initiation actually extended back to the bond program described in Chapter 6. Priority-fixing was formally done by the officials of the Housing Authority, but most of the influentials under study had to make their own allocations of values. These allocations were determined partly through informal meetings and contacts; the key meeting of the advisory citizens committee was a leading example. The major phase of this issue, however, was the promotional one. In fact, since its inception and approval at the time of the bond program, the major emphasis of the urban-renewal program in Atlanta has been on trying to gain acceptance.

Attributed and prescribed influentials were, after the initial decision, increasingly drawn into the fairly small core of those who had been trying to implement urban renewal and public housing—mainly professional and lay government officials. This activation reached its height in the public-housing site controversy. Both attributed and prescribed influentials came to play promotional roles, often in concert. Both public and "behind the scenes" endeavors marked this promotional work. Legitimation, which consisted of both a rejection and an acceptance of the proponents' plans came in aldermanic votes. Implementation continues to be a troublesome phase in Atlanta. With the exception of making financial contributions to the mayoralty campaign, the economic dominants remained true to type and did not figure prominently in either of these issues.

One of the most striking differences between these two issues and those described in the preceding chapter is in the emphases on utilizing resources for gaining acceptance—the promotional phase. By definition, this phase should be more prominent in controversial issues. In examples of veto power and the bond program, this phase was not attended by much involvement among the status-holders. More important, the level of intensity of the controversial issues was heightened considerably in the promotional stages. This heightening was especially noticeable in the urban renewal-public housing conflict, where "face-to-face" attempts at interpersonal influence were numerous.

Certainly, a major conclusion emerging from our discussion in these two chapters is that many attributed and prescribed influentials actually do play determinative decision-making roles and do exercise forms of power in community issues. Additionally, a large majority of the key actors came from these two groups. Conversely, those actors in our study who have no particular status as *political influentials*—the economic dominants—played minor decision-making roles and exercised little power in the specific issues discussed.

NOTES

1. That this pattern is not invariable, however, was demonstrated in 1962 by the defeat of a large bond proposal sponsored by Mayor Ivan Allen, Jr. His failure apparently stemmed from several causes—one important factor being that the Negro community did not lend the kind of support it had provided for the bond vote of 1957. A new proposal passed in 1963.

2. Ralph McGill, "You'd Think He Owns Atlanta," *Saturday Evening Post,* October 31, 1953, p. 29.

3. For an illustration of how "power centers" in the community shaped one electoral contest at the congressional level, see William J. Gore and Robert L. Peabody, "The Functions of the Political Campaign: A Case Study," *Western Political Quarterly,* XI (March, 1958), 55-70.

4. The oft-mentioned link between Hartsfield and Woodruff has gained rather wide belief. See, for example, Seymour Freedgood, "Life in Buckhead," *Fortune,* (September, 1961), p. 111. On the other hand, it appears that much of Woodruff's supposed influence was based on Hartsfield's "anticipating" his reactions.

5. Alexander later left his post, and the same observer noted, "He has since resigned his chairmanship and, so far as I can tell . . . , the Committee has gone the way of most committees, and is now effective on paper only."

6. The mayor apparently did not exert pressure until quite late in the controversy. As noted before, he had avoided rapid progress in the urban-renewal arena. Only when the issue was clear cut did he seek to persuade opposing aldermen to change their sentiments.

8

THE RULING ELITE

RE-EXAMINED*

WITH THE DATA presented so far, we are now in a position to make some general statements about political statuses and political roles in relation to two central questions about Atlanta's power structure—questions that also permeate much of the literature on community power structures. First, Is there a ruling elite that dominates decision-making in Atlanta? Second, If there is such an elite, is it composed primarily of economic dominants? The second question can be expanded into How much influence in general do the economic dominants wield?

A Second Look at the Ruling Elite

The most common way of identifying an alleged ruling elite is by the reputational approach, the central procedure Hunter used in his earlier work on Atlanta (*Community Power Structure*). His conclusion pointed toward a fairly gen-

*Portions of this chapter are drawn from the author's "Atlanta's Ruling Elite Revisited," in William J. Gore, *Reader in Decision-Making,* presented for publication.

eral ruling elite, dominated by leading businessmen, bound by common values, and acting in concert.

There are two primary means for testing this ruling-elite model. One is to use the reputational approach and then to investigate intensively the decision-making roles of the persons designated. If their behavior does indicate a pattern of decision-making by a ruling elite, then Hunter's model would be validated. If not, then the model would have to be questioned. A second means is adoption of an altogether different approach—such as a series of systematic case studies—from which would be derived a model of major decision-making. Again, the results can be compared with Hunter's findings.[1] Elements of both approaches were used in the present study. An inherent limitation of both types is in the time dimension. If later findings differ from earlier ones, for example, it can be argued that the structure has changed in the intervening years. We shall deal with this problem later.

Since the reputational approach was used in compiling our list of attributed influentials, we may ask whether or not this group does, in fact, compose a ruling elite similar to the one that Hunter described in earlier years. More specifically, we shall center our attention on the first-level attributed influentials. A majority of the institutional position-holders included in Hunter's list are also among the first-level attributed influentials of our study. These twenty-three people (including three who were not formally interviewed) may be viewed as a close equivalent of Hunter's twenty-seven "top leaders."

It is axiomatic that the more fully a group of men exerts pervasive, dominating influence on all major community policy-making, the more correctly the community is described as a ruling elite system. If the ruling-elite model is to be confirmed, therefore, the tests must demonstrate cohesive generalized influence among the supposed members. Furthermore, the influence of other actors in the system must be shown to be generally less than that of the reputed elite.

On the basis of simple politicization and scope of politicized roles, we should be inclined to reject the notion of a ruling elite for Atlanta. To be sure, the data in Chapters 4 and 5 demonstrate that the attributed influentials, especially those of the first echelon, are highly politicized and tend to be involved in a moderate range of issue-areas. There are two factors, however, that lessen the relevance of this behavior as support for the ruling-elite thesis. First, despite the fact that most attributed influentials were engaged in a moderate number of issues, there were considerable gaps. Participation was low in some areas— the virtual impossibility of monitoring and exercising control over the whole range of problems facing a rapidly growing metropolis like Atlanta militates against pervasive participation by even these highly politicized individuals. For example, on three major issues confronting the community, it was found that 35% of the first-level attributed influentials were highly involved in none or only one of the issues.

A second, more important factor is that certain other actors were found to be highly politicized also. The prescribed influentials, especially the government officials, engaged in behavior likely to produce consequential effects on issues almost as often—sometimes more often—than the attributed influentials. Because of the key institutional posts most of them hold, they are, furthermore, likely to have sizable constituencies as sources of strength. Then, too, their expertise often gives them opportunities to help shape alternatives by advice-giving. If the involvement and participation of the reputed elite are still considered high enough to conform to the ruling-elite model (an arguable point), then comparable behavior by the government officials and civic-staff personnel must also be recognized as satisfying the criteria. The result is that the circle of the nominal elite would be broken by "outsiders."

Although participation data provide some useful clues as to whether a ruling elite exists in Atlanta, they are by no means adequate, since they do not show the *consequences* of participation. There could conceivably be high participation but little influence (but not the reverse if we mean intended influence). Given their institutional positions, the economic and political resources at their command, their experience in community affairs, and the absence of highly divisive elements in the community, it is unlikely that that would be the case with the perceived and prescribed elites of Atlanta. Nevertheless, we must be more specific about resolution of community issues.

Our case studies provided the opportunity to assess more directly the influence of the actors under study. They also provided a test of the ruling-elite model. In discussing the case studies, the decision-making process was divided into five stages

—initiation, fixing priorities, gaining acceptance, legitimation, and implementation. These stages may be considered pivotal roles in the sense that the roles permitted or prevented major subsequent action and were not roles of a pro forma variety. It is here that involvement blends into influence, that is, achieving preferred outcomes or preventing others from achieving theirs. As the case studies unfolded, it was pointed out which status-occupants were performing which kinds of role and exercising which types of power.

This conception of decision-making places a premium on a rather extensive range of behaviors that influence the outcomes of community issues. It assigns relatively equal weight to various acts that contribute to issue resolution, although all have already been scrutinized to be sure they are at least consequential acts. One reason for adopting this conception is that influence and power, rather than leadership itself, were the subjects of study.

Another reason is that, on an issue of community-wide concern in a system where interests, power resources, and their utilization is moderate to high, it seems unlikely that actors will very often completely achieve their preferred outcomes. It is an over-simplification to speak of achieving outcomes as if each actor attains everything he seeks. Only when there is complete lack of opposition or of significant interests that must be considered, can we ordinarily say that an actor achieves his absolute preference on a given issue. Here is one reason why power has been defined as a phenomenon of purposive behavior that produces certain consequences, regardless of the actor's ultimate desire. It is often difficult, in fact, to ascertain ultimate perferences. As Harry Scoble has noted, "Correlations of policy preferences of an individual with actual outcomes in the issue (s) are probably poor measures of power because systems of partial power encourage participants to make excessive demands to gain what they are willing to settle for."[2]

The enactment of pivotal roles and the use of forms of power were sketched for two moderately significant issues and examined in detail for three major issues in Atlanta. On the lesser issues, it was found that an attributed influential (the mayor) and a prescribed influential (the water-works manager) exercised the main veto power against fluoridation. In the Community Chest crisis involving the Urban League, the key actors came primarily from the ranks of the attributed influentials. Because of the relatively circumscribed nature of these issues, and because of the lack of data in depth, these two issues do not provide very satisfactory tests of the ruling-elite model. The three major issues are much better tests.

A fair assumption is that the presence of a ruling elite varies directly with monopolization by one group of the pivotal roles that determine outcomes of major community issues. Let us call those who perform such roles *key actors*. If the attributed influentials had dominated the composition of the key actors in the three issues, then the case for this presumed elite would be strong. As Table 20 shows, however, the degree of

Table 20. Extent to Which Attributed Influentials Were Key Actors in the Resolution of Three Issues

| | ISSUES | | |
Key Actors	Bond Program	Mayoralty Election	Urban Renewal
First-level attributed influentials			
Number	7	15	7
Per cent*	16	39	19
Second-level attributed influentials			
Number	10	7	7
Per cent	23	18	19
Combined totals of attributed influentials			
Number	17	22	14
Per cent*	40	57	38
Nonattributed influentials			
Number	26	16	22
Per cent*	60	43	62
Total key actors			
Number	43	38	36
Per cent*	100	100	100

*Percentages are based on total number of key actors in each issue (next to last row of table).

monopolization of these pivotal roles varied for the three issues. In terms of our test, it is significant that the first-level attributed influentials (*the* reputed elite) provided less than one-fifth of the key actors on two of the three issues and only about two-fifths on the third. Only on the mayoralty issue did the combination of first- and second-level attributed influentials constitute a majority of the key actors.

Of equal significance is the composition of the rest of the key actors in the three issues. From about one-half to three-fourths were prescribed influentials. The small remainder belonged in neither the reputed nor the prescribed groups. The presence of nonattributed influential actors is a fundamental point. From that point and the fact that the first-level attributed elite failed to provide even a majority of key actors, we have conclusive evidence that members of the attributed elite do not come close to exclusive domination of the pivotal roles.

For analytical purposes, we have assumed roughly equal amounts of influence for various of these pivotal roles in three different issues. It is true, of course, that, even within this small universe of actors and types of behavior, some persons exercised more power than did others. Our aim, however, was not to rank the actors according to power exercised in these three issues studied. Rather it was to isolate the *major* actors in a more general sense. Had a ranking been attempted, the top-level attributed influentials might have held a modest, though not decisive, edge over the other groups.

Although the reputed elite did not dominate decision-making in the three issues considered separately, it is conceivable that a sizable proportion of them were key actors in all three issues.

Table 21. Number of Issues in Which Attributed Influentials Were Key Actors

Number of Issues	FIRST-LEVEL ATTRIBUTED INFLUENTIALS (N = 23)*	SECOND-LEVEL ATTRIBUTED INFLUENTIALS (N = 34)
None	35%	53%
One	26	26
Two	26	18
Three	13	3

*The Ns shown for both first- and second-level influentials in this table are slightly larger than in previous tabulations because of the inclusion of the four persons not interviewed.

Those who were key actors in one issue could also have been key actors in one or both of the others. If that were so, the claim of control by a general elite would be strengthened, since pervasive power is one condition for existence of such an elite. Table 21 indicates, however, that the overlap of key actors on all three issues is quite low, as it also is on two issues. Again, the upper-level attributed elite exhibit a greater proportion of multiple-issue influence than do their second-level colleagues. Significantly, the modal number of both first- and second-level attributed influentials actually failed to emerge as key actors on *any* of the issues. We should also note here that issue-overlap among members of the prescribed elite was no higher than among the attributed elite. There is no justification for claiming that they constitute any sort of general ruling elite either.

Discussion of Conflicting Findings

This material indicates how Atlanta's nominal ruling elite was subjected to a test of the ruling-elite model, a model which emerged from Hunter's original investigations. Viewed out of context and not in comparison with other actors, this group, especially its top echelon, seems to fit the configuration of a general elite. When other actors and the specifics of issue resolution are introduced into the analysis, however, the validity of the ruling-elite model appears more doubtful. That is not to say that the power structure of Atlanta is not perhaps more highly structured and less fragmented than those of some other communities.[3] In general, the upper echelons of Atlanta's power structure may be described as a number of slightly to moderately competitive coalitions, *not dominated by economic notables,* exercising determinative influence in their own policy areas. There is, in turn, a moderate amount of overlapping membership among these coalitions, with some actors performing interstitial roles in linking the coalitions.

Despite this *caveat,* a discrepancy clearly exists between our more recent findings and Hunter's original ones. There are at least three possible major causes for the discrepancy: change in the structure over time; different study orientations to the decision-making process; and questions of validation of the sociometric techniques. The most obvious possibility is that the configuration of power has changed in the approximately eight years that elapsed between the two research efforts.[4] There is some support for this explanation, especially in the increasing importance of local government officials in Atlanta and surrounding Fulton County. As federal programs in such fields as urban renewal, highway construction, housing, and airport development assume increasing importance in Atlanta's economic and political life, government officials speak more authoritatively on these subjects and are more often those who deal directly with state and national officials. They assume the role of influential specialists and help to fragment the distribution of power.

Developments in the field of race relations have also altered the distribution of power in recent years. Since the 1954 Supreme Court decision, Atlanta officials have been expected to take the lead in defining the ground rules of the local racial struggle. By the same token, Negroes have obtained increasing leverage in community decision-making. Negro voters have cast the "decisive" ballots in recent elections. The militant Negro student-protest movement in Atlanta has coincided with other developments to alter the patterns of influence in the larger community, as well as within the Negro community itself.

Of the possible reasons for discrepancies between the two pictures of Atlanta's power structure, change over time is the hardest to refute since precise reconstruction of the power structure of eight years ago is a difficult feat. The time explanation is at least questionable, however, because there have been no dramatic, overt changes in the structure similiar to that in northern cities like Philadelphia and New Haven and no radical policy innovations outside the race-relations area. The major institutions of the community are basically the same. The configuration of the current power structure seems based on the same sources as that in the past. Internal analysis of Hunter's work[5] and reliance on the informed opinion of participants and observers[6] provide other arguments against acceptance of Hunter's original formulations. On the basis of these arguments, it does not appear that the power structure has changed so much as the discrepancy between the two sets of findings suggests.

A second possible explanation for the inconsistency is that Hunter's orientation to decision-making and power is basically different from our own. Although his meaning is somewhat unclear, he seems to designate one pivotal stage in the decision-making continuum as determinative of all future events.[7] This stage is similar to our own second stage—fixing priorities. This orientation tends to emphasize the importance of dinner gatherings, telephone conversations, and office conclaves that are *presumably* necessary to make projects "go," to veto others, and to hold the *status quo* on still others. This orientation tends to overlook other phases and actors in the decision-making process —phases like initiation, planning, long range conditioning of attitudes, persuasion, bargaining, promotion, and implementation; and actors like civic-staff personnel, government officials, lay leaders, controllers of mass media, and episodic participants. By emphasizing one particular phase of decision-making, Hunter highlighted the importance of the attributed influentials. Our orientation placed no *a priori* emphases on any particular point in community decision-making (but did assume a continuum). Our study therefore highlights other roles performed by actors who are not necessarily perceived as influentials.

Third, the question arises about the validity of Hunter's portrayal of a unidimensional power structure. His severest critics charge that he committed the sin of reifying his concepts of power, influence, leadership, and decision-makers without actually demonstrating that the perceived influentials did exert pervasive influence on the resolution of vital issues in Atlanta. Specifically, it has been suggested that Hunter used one or more variants of three false tests of a ruling elite that Robert Dahl has suggested:

The first improper test confuses a ruling elite with a group that has a high *potential for control* . . . . The second improper test confuses a ruling elite with a group of individuals who have more influence than any others in the system. . . . The third improper test . . . is to generalize from a single scope of influence.[8]

Textual criticism of *Community Power Structure* yields evidence that Hunter did indeed use these false tests.[9] Certainly Atlanta's attributed elite, both then and now, lends itself to such improper tests. Virtually all its members occupy positions that vest incumbents with potential power; most do have more influence than most other people in the community; and most are influential in at least one policy area of community life. Our research attempted to avoid these three misleading tests by gaining more exact data on involvement and exercise of power-oriented behavior through detailed interviewing and case analysis. Perhaps, then, the differences in the two studies' conclusions arise from differences in the techniques of validating the nomination-attribution approach to identifying community decision-makers.

Our findings about Atlanta's power structure point toward a revision of Hunter's ruling-elite model. There is more specialization and therefore less generalization of decision-making among the reputed elite. Second, influentials are not restricted to the perceived elite. We do not reject, however, the claim that some actors are influential in more than one issue-area in the community. Influentials do overlap issue-areas in Atlanta, but the overlap is less extensive than Hunter implied and actors other than the reputed elite play key roles in decision-making.

From a methodological point of view, our findings show that the nomination-attribution technique is neither so infallible as its supporters claim nor so misleading as its attackers insist. Most of the perceived influentials at both levels were indeed influential in one or more issue areas. Those considered most influential tended to engage in more deliberately influential behavior and appeared actually to be more influential than those reputed to be less influential. The technique measures more than simply respect, popularity, or social status. It serves to locate people of consequence in community decision-making.

Two results of our study illustrate the limitations of the technique, however. First, few deductions can be made about the scope, nature, and employment of the influence of the attributed influentials. Few were found to be actively engaged in a majority of the issues and issue-areas cited and a few were mostly inactive. The researcher cannot conclude that, because others perceive them as generally influential, they actually are generally influential. In fact, it appears that they are usually engaged in a restricted number of areas. Second, the finding that actors other than those perceived as community influentials also become involved in and play key roles in issue resolution disproves the claim that the reputed elite monopolizes community decision-making. After such an elite has been defined, it remains an empirical question whether its members "run" the community.

The Place of the Economic Dominants

If, indeed, there is no general ruling elite in Atlanta, the question of whether the economic dominants constitute this elite is eliminated. Even though we reject the notion of a ruling

elite composed of economic notables, however, it is still worth-
while to re-examine Hunter's conclusion that the economic
giants are the linchpins of Atlanta's power structure.

Taking only those economic dominants who were not also
attributed influentials—twenty-six of the forty-one identified—the
data clearly show them to be less politicized than the attributed
and prescribed influentials on virtually all measures. More significantly, almost none appeared as key actors in the resolution
of our two minor and three major issues. Surely, if they composed even a modest ruling elite, they would have emerged as
key actors in at least one and preferably all of these issues.

This test is a bit unfair since it excludes those fifteen economic dominants who were also among the fifty-seven attributed
influentials. Their behavior can be summarized as reflecting the
general behavior of the attributed influentials as a whole. For
example, if one-third of the attributed influentials exhibited a
certain behavioral characteristic, then probably about one-third
of the fifteen economic dominants within that group would
exhibit the same characteristic. This statement is, of course, a
rough rule of thumb that would not apply in all instances.
An examination of the evidence, however, provides no clues to
suggest a consistent differentiation between the economic dominants among the attributed influentials and the attributed influentials as a whole.

Where, then, is the place of the economic dominants in
the power structure? The answer is in two parts. First, the
economic dominants of Atlanta are only one of several key
groups that play significant roles in community decision-making. Both elective and appointive government officials, both professional and amateur civic-staff personnel, and a variety of other
actors form the total *dramatis personae* of most community issues. There is no evidence to suggest that the economic dominants
who do exercise power consistently or often prevail over other
actors.

Second, the economic dominants are by no means a monolithic group in terms of their behavior. This point is most
apparent in the tremendous differences in the power-oriented
activities they engage in. As the evidence shows, this behavior
falls at the lower end of the continuum among those not perceived as influential but edges into the upper end among those
who are perceived as influential. Far less than a majority of the

economic dominants are key actors in community decision-making in Atlanta, but those who are share power with other elites.

Having established that the economic dominants as a class do not form a ruling group, nevertheless we cannot deny the importance some of them have for decision-making in Atlanta. It is apparent, for example, that economic interests and leaders are more influential in Atlanta than in Chicago, New York, and New Haven, to mention three cities that have been thoroughly explored in the literature.[10] Their influence is more akin to that reported in such cities as Detroit, Seattle, Pittsburgh, Dallas, and perhaps Syracuse.[11]

Why are economic dominants more influential in Atlanta than in some other American cities? Very briefly, we may sketch in three possible reasons.[12] First, the governmental and partisan structure of Atlanta is conducive to civic-political activity on the part of economic interests. There is an absence of political party organization and control at the local level. Elections are, in effect, nonpartisan, so that the business leaders whose tendencies are Republican at the national level are not bothered by supporting candidates who in most instances are Democrats. More important, since they do not have to work through a party apparatus that might be repugnant to them, the economic leaders are able to enter the fray of candidate selection and support directly, if often covertly. The absence of strong partisanship not only encourages initial engagement, but it also means that the presence of a strong coalition of partisan interests—like that of Chicago—is not present as a competitor for power and influence in the day-to-day issues facing the community. Economic interests are thus more likely to have an influential voice, and are thereby encouraged to participate still further. The presence of a formally weak and decentralized city and county government has also proved conducive to the exertion of economic power.

The second reason is related to the characteristics of the firms with which many of the leading economic notables are associated. As shown in Chapter 3, economic dominants who are perceived as influentials (and who in fact tend to *be* influential) most often come from locally owned, downtown firms with a locus of consumption in the immediate metropolitan area. The futures of their firms are thus tied firmly to the future of the community. There is, in short, a tremendous incentive to participate. Nor should we discount the incentives coming from more altruistic and traditional sources. Many of these economic dominants come from families and firms for which service to the community has been a responsibility for decades. To some extent, today's actors have internalized these civic-obligation norms.

Such incentives would not be sufficient, however, were the "climate" for business influence less favorable in Atlanta. One of the factors here is the prevailing ideology in the community, an ideology that has served to heighten the hospitality of the decision-making structure to action by economic interests.

The absence of a strong working-class movement and organization, the exclusion of "redneck" and "woolhat" elements from the upper levels of decision-making, and the aforementioned absence of party operations have all served the cause of the business ethic and business spirit in the community. Furthermore, leading economic institutions have not treated the community and its inhabitants badly. If a spirit of *noblesse oblige* has guided some of their actions, it has not caused resentment. Partly because they have developed some imposing economic giants of their own, the Negroes of the community have, until recently, directed little of their fire against the business elements of the community.

While there are incentives and a favorable climate for some economic notables, still a third ingredient is essential: relatively high cohesion among diverse economic enterprises. Financial, real-estate, construction, and retail firms have often acted with a unanimity rare in other communities. If industry has seldom been part of this alliance, it is not from opposition so much as from disinterest. One factor producing cohesion lies in institutional arrangements like the strong Chamber of Commerce and satellite organizations. There are no competing civic-business organizations, although some trade organizations may find themselves at odds from time to time. Cohesion is also based on personal ties, many of them stretching back over two or three generations. "Gut-fighting" is not likely to flourish in this environment.

Another source of cohesion is the role of a half-dozen or so economic firms as pace setters and opinion leaders for other members of the large business interests. Thanks to their resources, the efficiency with which they use them, and their generally good personal relations with others, these opinion leaders help weld the business community into a united front. Finally, for a complex series of reasons, Atlanta business leaders seem to feel that all will profit in the long run from benefits that may not be apparent for any one given firm. There is a feeling that another firm's gain is not necessarily one's own loss.

Some of these explanations of why some economic leaders are quite influential in Atlanta could be applied, with certain changes, to explaining why Atlanta has a more pluralistic power structure than the one Hunter attributed to it. Economic dominants, elective and appointive government officials, lay and professional civic leaders, and minority group leaders—especially from the Negro community—all have some say in who rules and what is decided in Atlanta.[13]

NOTES

1. This test is essentially the one proposed by Robert A. Dahl in "A Critique of the Ruling Elite Model," *American Political Science Review,* LII (June, 1958), 406. The two tests are not necessarily mutually exclusive, and, in fact, they complement each other. Of the two, however, the first is simpler, for it entails study only of the behavior of one defined population, rather than research into a specific decision-making process and ferreting out of all the influentials. Its liability is that it satisfactorily provides only for rejection of the model. If a substantial portion of the presumed elite was not influential in decision-making, the model can be rejected. But if all or most of them were influential in resolving issues, this does not necessarily mean that other actors in the system were not also influential, unless the research has been specifically designed to seek such evidence.

2. Harry Scoble, "Leadership Hierarchies and Political Issues in a New England Town," in Morris Janowitz, ed., *Community Political Systems* (New York: The Free Press of Glencoe, 1961), p. 136.

3. For two journalistic accounts that suggest high concentrations of influence in Atlanta, see Douglass Cater, "Atlanta: Smart Politics and Good Relations," *The Reporter* (July 11, 1957), pp. 18-21; and Seymour Freedgood, "Life in Buckhead," *Fortune* (September, 1961), pp. 108-14+.

4. In one of the few instances in the literature of the social sciences of the empirical re-examination of reported findings, the time factor was found to explain some, but by no means all, of the discrepancies. Our reference is to Robert Redfield, *Tepoztlan: A Mexican Village* (Chicago: University of Chicago Press, 1930); and to Oscar Lewis, *Life in a Mexican Village: Tepoztlan Restudied* (Urbana: University of Illinois Press, 1951). For a discussion of these two studies, see Horace Miner, "The Folk-Urban Continuum," *American Sociological Review,* XVII (October, 1952), 529-37. More relevant to our work are two studies of Syracuse, New York. Wayne Hodges, in *Company and Community* (New York: Harper & Row, Publishers, 1958), found that industrialists in locally owned firms were at the apex of the

power structure and government officials and politicians were subordinate. A later study—Roscoe C. Martin, Frank J. Munger, *et al., Decisions in Syracuse* (Bloomington: Indiana University Press, 1961)—encompassed part of the time period covered by Hodges. The conclusions were quite different, with a variety of actors and institutions appearing as power wielders. Differences in methodology and orientation appear to account for the variance between the two studies.

5. See particularly Raymond Wolfinger, "Reputation and Reality in the Study of Community Power," *American Sociological Review*, XXV (October, 1960), 636-44; Herbert Kaufman and Victor Jones, "The Mystery of Power," *Public Administration Review*, XIV (Summer, 1954), 205-12. For a detailed dissection of the famous Middletown studies, parts of which resemble Hunter's, see Nelson Polsby, "Power in Middletown: Fact and Value in Community Research," *Canadian Journal of Economics and Political Science*, XXVI (November, 1960), 592-603.

6. Although no systematic effort was made to gather such opinion, several respondents questioned the validity of the ruling-elite model for Atlanta.

7. Floyd Hunter, *Community Power Structure* (Chapel Hill: University of North Carolina Press, 1953), pp. 95-100.

8. Dahl, *op. cit.,* p. 645.

9. See note 5.

10. See Edward C. Banfield, *Political Influence* (New York: The Free Press of Glencoe, 1961), Wallace S. Sayre and Herbert Kaufman, *Governing New York City* (New York: Russell Sage Foundation, 1960), and Robert A. Dahl, *Who Governs?* (New Haven: Yale University Press, 1961) for reports on Chicago, New York, and New Haven, respectively.

11. For a report on Detroit's business leaders, see [author anonymous] in David Greenstone, *A Report on Politics in Detroit* (Cambridge: Joint Center for Urban Studies of the Massachusetts Institute of Technology and Harvard University, 1961), Part V, 1-19. Two studies of Seattle are Delbert C. Miller, "Industry and Community Power Structure: A Comparative Study of an American and an English City," *American Sociological Review*, XXIII (February, 1958), 9-15; and William J. Gore and Robert L. Peabody, "The Functions of the Political Campaign: A Case Study," *Western Political Quarterly*, XI (March, 1958), 55-70. Pittsburgh is referred to in Peter B. Clark, "Civic Leadership: The Symbols of Legitimacy," (paper delivered at the 1960 meeting of the American Political Science Association. New York, September, 1960). A recent account of Dallas is found in Carol Estes Thometz, *The Decision-Makers* (Dallas: Southern Methodist University Press, 1963). See Martin, Munger, *et al., op. cit.,* for data on Syracuse.

12. The organization of the following pages draws on [author anonymous] in Greenstone, *loc. cit.*

13. The reader will notice that little attention has been paid the average citizen and his part in decision-making. Obviously, the scope and design of the study did not permit any extensive work in this area. On the basis of what has been observed about the masses in Atlanta, however, it appears that they are probably no better or worse off than citizens of other metropolises when it comes to political participation, access to decision-making posts, and having their preferences anticipated by influentials.

9

STATUS

AND ROLE

ACQUISITION

Since political status in the community is not primarily a matter of prescription, the acquisition of high status and the roles associated with high status become topics for empirical question. What social processes inerest individuals in exercising political influence in the communty? By what initial role enactments are they introduced into the decision-making structure? By what hierarchies, if any, do they advance? Do they pass on their interest in community affairs to their offspring? These major questions are examined in this chapter. Because of the exploratory nature of this phase of the study, our findings and interpretations should be taken as speculative and tentative.

Political Socialization

Herbert Hyman, in his ground-breaking survey, examined political socialization in a number of different societies.[1] Socialization theory posits that certain patterns of behavior associated with positions in society are *learned* and that such behavior developed at a formative stage of life, usually the pre-adult years, serves to ensure continuity of these patterns through time, even though they may be modified.

Socialization is not confined to the early years, however. A broader view of socialization is that it is a process that can occur at various stages of life:

> The term socialization in its current usage in the literature refers primarily to the process of child development. This is in fact a crucially important case of the operation of what are here called the mechanisms of socialization, but it should be made clear that the term is here used in a broader sense than the current one to designate the learning of *any* orientations of functional significance to the operation of a system of complementary role-expectations. In this sense, socialization, like learning, goes on throughout life. The case of the development of the child is only the most dramatic because he has so far to go.[2]

A simple hypothesis about political socialization is that, the more politicized the child's parents, the more politicized will be the child. The evidence presented so far demonstrates that Atlanta's attributed and prescribed influentials are rather highly politicized in terms of community decision-making and the economic dominants much less so. Even though their middle and upper socio-economic class positions are a factor limiting generalization, these status-holders still present useful collectivities for testing the hypothesis. During the formal interviews, the respondents were asked one question bearing directly on this point: "In regard to community affairs would you say your father was (is) inactive, slightly active, fairly active, very active?"[3]

By dividing the subjects according to whether their fathers had been "inactive" or "slightly active" (low) and "fairly active" or "very active" (high), we can assess, in crude fashion, the relative importance of the direction of the political socialization. Surprisingly, the degree of the father's participation in community affairs appears to make only a slight difference in the present political status (and behavior) of the respondents. Among all groups, except the second-level perceived influentials (where the proportions were about equal), about three-fifths of the respondents came from homes where the fathers had high activity levels.

Despite the fact that they are by far the least politically oriented group, the economic dominants have almost as great a percentage of active fathers as do the other elites. In terms of their own activity, it makes little difference whether the economic dominants came from politicized homes. The involvement scores for community issues and activities vary little among the economic dominants, regardless of whether their fathers were active or inactive. These findings substantiate an earlier assertion about the economic notables: They, more than the other elites, stress social mobility rather than community influence. In their drive for socio-economic status, they tend to avoid extreme involvement in community decision-making. Despite highly active fathers, a majority of them seem to have sublimated this form of socialization.

Although direction of political socialization does not appear crucial in Atlanta, it may be more decisive for elites in other communities. Because of the dearth of material on political

Table 22. Comparison of Father's Community-Participation Level for Elites of Two Communities

| | FATHER'S ACTIVITY LEVEL | | | |
	Low	High	Total	Number
Attributed Influentials				
Atlanta	48%	52	100%	(52)
Raleigh	15%	85	100%	(34)
Prescribed Influentials				
Atlanta	39%	61	100%	(44)
Raleigh	26%	74	100%	(38)
Economic Dominants				
Atlanta	45%	55	100%	(20)
Raleigh	14%	86	100%	(22)

socialization, we shall rely heavily on comparative data from a similar study in Raleigh, North Carolina.[4] When the same question about the father's activity in community affairs was asked of a comparable range of elites in Raleigh, a strikingly different profile resulted. Table 22 shows the comparison between Atlanta and Raleigh data with the subclasses of the attributed influentials and the perceived influentials combined (the differences are small in each case) for each community to facilitate presentation.

Fathers proved more active for all classes in Raleigh, differing widely from data in Atlanta for the perceived influentials and the economic dominants. Without extensive analysis, we can still suggest some reasons why early socialization seems so much more common in Raleigh than in Atlanta. The type of community seems the most significant cause for the disparity between the two sets of attributed influentials. In contrast to large, cosmopolitan, economically booming Atlanta, Raleigh is a much more tradition-bound, slowly moving community. The traditional values of the smaller community may serve to elevate especially those whose parents have been active in the community, while such values are less consequential in the more dynamic and complex social structure of Atlanta. Despite the greater proportion of native attributed influentials in Atlanta, more of them came from homes where the fathers were not particularly active than was true of the Raleigh natives. Of the twenty-four Atlanta natives in this group, 54% of them had highly active fathers, while of the eleven Raleigh natives, 82% reported highly active fathers.[5]

Although differences in the social structures of the communities may explain these differences for the natives, how do we account for the differences in father's activity level among those who are not natives? There is no ready explanation. Evidently the decision-making structures elevate selectively these from outside the community. In part, the differentiation may be a product of the selective attraction the community holds for diverse types of individuals. Another possibility is that the structures of the two communities have different needs. One type of individual may be more functional for the structure of one community, another type for the other. It is also possible that simple chance is at work here.

As Table 22 indicates, the disparity between the prescribed influentials of the two communities is less than for the other elites, although activity level is still higher for the Raleigh fathers.

The difference between the two sets of economic dominants is virtually identical to that between the sets of attributed influentials. Despite their highly active fathers, the economic dominants of Raleigh are, according to comparable measures, even less politicized than those of Atlanta. We must suggest again the sublimation of early political socialization in striving for more material goals as part of the explanation for this phenomenon.

Another, more tangible factor may also be involved. A majority of the Raleigh economic dominants work with smaller and less well known commercial organizations. In Atlanta, the economic dominants are associated with larger, better known firms, mostly in manufacturing. It seems plausible that the firms located in the larger city choose and are chosen by upwardly mobile men from less privileged backgrounds than those associated with the commercial firms of Raleigh. Using father's occupation as an index, we can substantiate this suggestion. While 91% of the Raleigh economic dominants had fathers who were managers, proprietors, professionals, or farmer-owners, only 50% of the Atlanta economic dominants' fathers fell into these high-status categories.[6]

We thus find in the smaller city men of higher socio-economic origins whose fathers had fairly high levels of political activity. The sons have been imperfectly socialized, however, and have apparently substituted other goals or undergone negative reactions. In Atlanta, there are more men from poorer backgrounds, for whom economic mobility is a paramount consideration. Low politicization is the common denominator in both communities, however. The differences between this class in the two cities seems less a function of community structure than of the individual's strivings and the economic enterprise with which he becomes associated.

Introduction into the Structure

The decision-making structure of a community, like any structure, has ways of recruiting personnel to carry out its processes and its functions. This recruitment is directly connected to political socialization. How do actors receive their induction into the decision-making structure of the local community? How are they introduced into new roles? To reach at least a partial answer, we asked this question in the formal interviews: "Thinking back, what particular event or person would you single out as being most important for your becoming active in community affairs?" For those whose livelihoods were wrapped up in community activity, the question was interpreted as applying primarily to their recruitment into their governmental or staff positions.

Responses to this question are presented in Table 23. Most people cited a specific factor or factors through which they were recruited. A rather unusual note is that the attributed and

Table 23. Source of Induction into Community Affairs

	Attributed Influentials	Prescribed Influentials
Friends and associates	42% *	42%
Relatives	12	9
Occupational position	18	24
Drive or campaign	22	11
Organization	16	7
Personal predisposition	8	13
"Just happened"	6	11
Number	(50)	(45)

*Percentages do not total 100% because some respondents listed more than one source.

prescribed influentials vary little in the inducements they named. Let us scrutinize some of these factors.

Friends and associates far outrank family members. Recalling the slight association between level of father's activity and son's political status, the order is not surprising.[7] This is not to deny the importance of familial specialization for certain individuals, but the data suggest that for recruitment into community affairs the requests and demands of friends or associates are more persuasive and salient than are family experiences. Typically, the designated recruiter was an older person already active in community issues. A few Atlanta patriarchs were named repeatedly.

As for influential events, attainment of certain occupational positions proved the most salient. Some positions in Atlanta are natural sources of decision-making roles, not only because of their prestige value, but also because their incumbents are committed to active participation in order to enhance the outcomes of their firms. As one venerable executive of a downtown store commented:

I first became active when I gained a leading position in this firm. You can't be president here and not become involved in community issues. In my case I became particularly involved in streets and traffic problems. How can you separate the problems of the city from the problems of this store?

Certain expectations develop about the roles of some position-occupants, both in the community and in their firms. One mammoth service industry, for example, has a long record of presidents and board chairmen who devote considerable time (and their executives' time) to all types of community projects. Strategically located people in the community expect such expenditures of time, as does the firm itself.

Special drives and campaigns are the second most important type of event, whether they are of the fund-raising or the governmental type. Some people become fully active only in response to a drive or project that then serves to carry them on to other drives and projects. One person noted that he first became involved in community activities as a young lawyer. Participating in a welfare building project seemed to him an idealistic, yet personally useful way, of increasing his law practice. He said, "After my success in that drive, I have been in on every major welfare drive in Atlanta." Others report different forms of initiation: "The event which really got me into community activities was my decision to run for city alderman against a man whom I had words with." Another said, "Being selected to be on the local government commission ten years ago was the vital event."

A third source of induction is membership or office-holding in an organization, usually of a civic nature. A second-level perceived influential remarked that:

Originally some friend of mine asked me to join the Junior Chamber of Commerce. In a few years I was president of the organization. Then the mayor asked me to run for city alderman. I guess joining the Chamber was the real event which got me started.

People view high activity levels from slightly different perspectives, based in part upon the levels at which they currently act in the decision-making structure. One widely perceived influential remarked "Well, the event that started me operating at this level was being made president of the Chamber of Commerce." His whole experience in that organization had activated him. Another person replied, "I guess my being asked to join the

Y.M.C.A. during the depression to get it out of bankruptcy was the leading event."

Another set of induction procedures involves personal pre-dispositions. A few individuals answered that they had always been interested in community affairs. They could not single out any person (even a family member) or event that had led them into community activities. For example, a civic-staff official (nonprofessional) declared, "No, there was no special event; I just feel that I would like to carry my load as a citizen." A note of altruism marks these responses.

Finally, eight status-holders said they could neither single out a person or an event as significant, nor claim personal pre-dilection. As one person said, "There doesn't seem to be any one person or thing; I just drifted into it." Actually, of course, interpersonal influence or the impact of an event probably did precipitate participation. In retrospect, however, such factors are apparently not significant to respondents. This type of re-sponse is empirically similar to that of "personal predisposition."

As explained earlier, there are three major arenas of deci-sion-making in Atlanta—governmental, fund-raising, and private. The most important decisions are made in the governmental sphere. How significant are the events or people associated with these major games in terms of role-induction? To assess their importance, we classified them according to whether they origi-nated in the governmental sphere. Some knowledge of the characteristics of the named individuals and the circumstances surrounding named events was necessary. Fortunately, a major-ity of the individuals and events named were of fairly well known local origin. This familiarity facilitated the classification.

The classification yielded the following percentages who attested to induction via the government arena:

First-level attributed influentials 50%
Second-level attributed influentials 30%
Government officials 56%
Civic staff 27%
Economic dominants 7%

Not unexpectedly, the economic dominants rate lowest on this scale. Those economic dominants who are active in community affairs tend to specialize in private and fund-raising activities and to engage in a minimum of public issues. Their interests are thus compatible with their activating sources.

The relatively high percentage of government-oriented activation reported by the government officials also conforms to expectations. The professionals in this group compose the bulk of the 56%. They frequently reported either acceptance of their positions or other government officials associated with them as the causes of their entries into community activities. One professional said:

The head of the Atlanta_____Authority resigned. Because I was with the federal government counterpart here in Atlanta, that gave me access to the position. That's when I automatically became involved in community problems.

Some of the nonprofessionals also reported initial recruitment by public actors or events. A recently appointed lay board chairman serving in a controversial issue-area commented simply, "The mayor." A state legislator explained that the growing problems and complexity of his county prompted him to run for office.

The rather high incidence of top-level attributed influentials who were initiated via the government arena is not so easily explained. We might expect these high-status (both politically and socio-economically) influentials to have been initiated into community activities primarily through the fund-raising or private spheres, which are indeed avenues frequently used in the community, as we shall see. But the most salient factor for one-half this group was a government issue or personality. A banker commented:

Because of my financial position I became involved in the reorganization of the city's finances back in 19—. Then I became interested in public-housing development in the city. From there on my interests spread into other areas.

Another cited an electoral contest:

Well, the thing that really got me interested was the mayor's second-term try. I just couldn't stay out of that one.

Others noted the influence of their families or associates, which had quickened their interests and desires to participate. Although the stimulus is not so directly related to occupation as with the government officials, the banker who became involved in public-housing development because of his occupational position is not rare. A newspaper editor, for example, commented that he had a lively interest in politics. Then, as an afterthought, he added, "You have to in the newspaper game."

Slightly over one-fourth of the civic-staff personnel and the second-level attributed influentials cited a recruitment source in the governmental arena. Among the former, the nonprofessionals are more likely to have been initiated *via* governmental projects or people. A young lawyer said, "My work involves me so much with city officials that I cannot avoid being drawn in on various public projects." One of the voting-organization leaders commented:

My whole family has been in politics for a long time. Then too, I went to college during the depression. This had a profound effect on my views about political participation, far different than present college generations.

One professional did fall into this category:

I decided to run for the state legislature way back in 19—. Although I was defeated, this event opened up a broad interest in community affairs. I've been in the business ever since.

The civic-staff people citing nongovernmental recruitment tended to be professionals or others who had been activated by associates or occupational factors not governmentally oriented.

Six of the nine second-level attributed influentials who named a governmental source were themselves government officials—indication that their original stimulus has carried over into overt politicized behavior in the form of holding public offices. One of them referred to a negative factor that caused his participation:

I first got interested in community politics because I was so disgusted with the corrupt politics of the Pendergast machine in Kansas City. I thought a community could be better run than that.

Three respondents mentioned Mayor Hartsfield. Said one:

The important event for me was being assigned to the city-hall beat for the paper. There I grew to know and admire the mayor. This relationship has been important to me.

Although most community decision-making studies have not explored the political socialization of actors in the system, the work of Heinz Eulau and his associates[8] sheds some light on this process among the legislators of four states. Their study provides some interesting comparative material about political socialization among different kinds of influentials. By recasting our response categories, we arrive at an organization of data roughly comparable to theirs.[9] To facilitate presentation, the data for the four state legislative bodies are combined, as are those for the prescribed and attributed influentials within Atlanta and Raleigh.

Table 24 demonstrates that the ranking of socializing fac-

Table 24. Relative Importance of Induction Sources for State Legislators and for Influentials of Two Communities, by Rank and Percentage

	STATE LEGISLATORS*		ATLANTA		RALEIGH	
	Rank	Per cent**	Rank	Per cent	Rank	Per cent
Participation	1	54	3	27	2	33
Predisposition	2	48	4	11	4	14
Primary group	3	41	1	51	1	47
Events or conditions	4	26	2	32	3	30
Beliefs	5	5	5	0	5	0
Number		(494)		(95)		(70)

*Tabulated from data in Heinz Eulau, et al., "The Political Socialization of American State Legislators," in Eulau, et al., eds., Legislative Behavior: A Reader in Theory and Research (New York: The Free Press of Glencoe, 1959), p. 311.

**Percentages in each column do not total 100% because some actors listed more than one source.

tors operating on state legislators is quite different from that for political actors in the two communities. Primary groups are most important for community influentials, while participation is most important for state legislators. Another striking contrast is that between high personal predisposition at the community level and low at the state level. The great similarity between the two communities' rankings—the percentages are within five points of each other for each category—indicates that similar processes may introduce actors into the decision-making structure, regardless of inter-community differences.

It cannot, of course, be claimed that the state legislators and the community influentials are comparable in composition. The state legislator competes for and occupies a political office. About one-fifth of the status-holders in Atlanta and Raleigh occupy such offices (too low a frequency to justify comparisons on the basis of elective positions). Actually, this dissimilarity sharpens the comparison because it indicates that different kinds of actors in political systems may derive their interests from different sources. What sets the politician running for the state legislature can be quite different, as the data suggest, from what stimulates the local influential.

The greater importance of primary groups for the local influential may be a product of his attempt to conform in his community role to the expectations of others, a factor that is not so important to the office-seeker. This observation is supported by the much greater importance of personal predisposition among the state legislators. The elected politician may be trying to fulfill personal goals, desires, and interests, while the local influential usually acts from a more pragmatic point of view.

Avenues to Influence Roles

We have more detailed information about the induction of actors into decision-making roles. In most organized endeavors, there is a series of steps that those at the apexes have traveled, barring lateral introduction. These steps generally take the form of career ladders in occupational endeavors. In nonprofit organizations, the process is popularly known as "going through the chairs." Community influentials may be expected to follow certain career lines. In this study we were particularly interested in the career lines of the attributed influentials because of their high political status in the eyes of others and because their careers are more likely to develop independently of organizational hierarchies than are those of the prescribed influentials. Instead of focusing on specific stages in these careers, we shall highlight various avenues through which attributed influentials come to play and maintain their decision-making roles.

To determine that such avenues exist in Atlanta, we asked the attributed influentials to list their major activities in five-year periods back to 1936. One aim was to ascertain in what kinds of activity these influentials first became involved. We established nine categories of activity for initiation into community affairs. The same procedures were employed in the Raleigh study.

Table 25 presents the percentages and rankings for initiatory

Table 25. Types of Initiatory Community Activity for Attributed Influentials, by Rank and Percentage

	ATLANTA		RALEIGH	
	Rank	Per cent*	Rank	Per cent
Welfare drives	1	43	2	34
Government affairs	2	33	3	31
Civic organizations	3	29	1	43
Professional organizations	4	16	8	6
Electoral	5	14	6	11
Service clubs	6	10	5.5	26
Social-cultural	7	8	9	3
Religious	8.5	6	5.5	26
Educational	8.5	6	7	9
Number		(49)		(39)

*Percentages do not total 100% because many actors reported more than one type of initiatory activity.

activities[10] in both communities. Three of the categories need further explanation. "Government affairs" means endeavors carried out primarily by or through government (public) agencies. The category is distinguished from electoral activity, which involves candidates competing for political posts or holding such posts. "Educational" means both private- and public-school activities.

The three leading avenues in each community are welfare drives, government affairs, and participation—usually holding office—in civic organizations. These three forms of activity are perhaps the most pervasively community oriented in American localities. For instance, one way that junior executives demonstrate their executive mettle is through participation in welfare drives of various types. As one Atlanta respondent proclaimed:

They don't appoint these fat cats to head up these drives for no reason. Not only do they lend prestige; they also have the manpower
to do a lot of the staff and leg work that has to be done in a big
drive. They can sign over some of their junior executives practically
half time for the duration.

In both communities, the art of drawing young executives into
the welfare-fund game has been developed almost to a science,
with a variety of inducements, training, and ego-recognition
techniques. Welfare-fund activity is normally an innocuous way
to be initiated into community affairs.

Much the same can be said of civic organizations. For business and social purposes, joining one or more of these groups
is not unusual. Both communities have a plethora of civic organizations that qualified residents may join; the Chamber of
Commerce was the most frequently mentioned in both.

Actors introduced through the public affairs avenue have
two alternatives, both of which involve appointments to various
public bodies. They may be initiated *via* temporary study commissions or *ad hoc* promotional committees, but more often they
come through membership in permanent lay boards. There is
no dearth of such boards in either community.

Although influentials in the two communities attribute
approximately equal importance to the three leading types of
introductory activity, the same is not true for the other types.
After the first three, the ranking for Atlanta actually shows
little percentage difference between professional organization
participation (ranked fourth at 16%) and educational and religious activities (ranked last in a tie at 6% each). Raleigh,
however, attaches greater importance to service clubs and church-
related activities. Why this difference between the two communities?

As we suggested before, Raleigh is a smaller, more homogeneous, and more provincial community than Atlanta. The
service clubs perform some of the functions that larger, better-
staffed civic associations perform in bigger communities. Then,
too, exercising leadership in one of the luncheon clubs is a
higher mark of distinction in a smaller community, where opportunities for leadership are more limited than in Atlanta,
for example.

The emphasis on church-related activities also seems more

typical of the smaller town, especially in the South. Perhaps it is a product of the importance attached to religious behavior and leadership. The higher esteem of religious values may serve as a basis for induction into still larger spheres of community decision-making.[11] Furthermore, the smaller the community, the greater the likelihood that various types of community-oriented church work will be important in the total scope of decision-making.

One characteristic of initiatory ventures is the wide dispersion by arena, even though there is a concentration in three types of activity for Atlanta and five for Raleigh. If we calculate the occurrence of all types of activity for all time periods, we should find an even larger and wider distribution in percentage terms, merely because an actor's scope is likely to increase the longer he participates, assuming that he is vertically or horizon-

Table 26. Distribution of Activity Types for Attributed Influentials in Two Communities over Extended Length of Time, by Rank and Percentage

	ATLANTA		RALEIGH	
	Rank	Per cent*	Rank	Per cent
Government affairs	1	76	3	60
Welfare drives	2	65	1	83
Civic organizations	3	57	2	69
Educational	4	33	7	26
Electoral	5.5	31	6	31
Professional organizations	5.5	31	9	14
Social-cultural	7	22	8	20
Religious	8.5	14	5	34
Service clubs	8.5	14	4	49
Number		(49)		(35)

*Percentages do not total 100% because most actors mentioned more than one activity.

tally mobile. To test this expectation, all types of activity mentioned at least once were counted, resulting in a total range of endeavors for each respondent throughout all time periods.

The data confirm the expectation (see Table 26). When compared with first-period activities shown in Table 25, the over-all distribution shows an increment in every category of activity. This increment occurs for each community and ranges from a low of 4% for service-club work in Atlanta to a high of 49% for welfare-drive participation in Raleigh.

These findings also underline the importance attributed to the three leading initiating spheres of action. In each instance in both communities, the percentages are approximately doubled. The participants, then, are almost inevitably drawn into one of these spheres during their careers. In Atlanta, the stronger pull is toward government affairs, while in Raleigh it is toward welfare drives.

We might conclude from the percentages in the government affairs category that many attributed influentials in both communities do not engage in issues upon which the legal governments and agents (including voters) are the final decision-makers. The error of this conclusion lies in the fact that several other categories include activities that are primarily governmental or political in character. Electoral and educational activities are obvious examples. Civic-organization work may not be so obvious. Serving as president of the Chamber of Commerce or some other major civic association inevitably entangles the office-holder in a variety of public issues, some of them minor, but many of them of consequence. To a more limited degree, behaviors associated with leadership in the service clubs and professional organizations also involve the individual in a host of quasi-political undertakings.

Three of the minor categories highlight trends first revealed by the initial-period activities. While nearly one-third of the Atlanta attributed influentials reported participation in professional organizations, only 14% of their Raleigh counterparts did so. This difference is partially a function of the different sizes of the two communities. More specialized and vital professional organizations are found in Atlanta than in Raleigh. Engineers and architects, for example, have much more flourishing organizations than their colleagues in Raleigh. Even more important, Atlanta's legal associations are more instrumental in the recruitment and socializing of influentials than are Raleigh's. Many upwardly mobile lawyers make a point of holding office in the city and county bar organizations. Atlanta's professional associations can generally make themselves felt; consequently, Atlanta actors view participation in these associations as a significant community endeavor.

Two other avenues that serve important career functions in Raleigh—service clubs and church-related work—receive little emphasis in the Georgia city, even when all time periods are considered. This difference in stress clearly transcends the initial role-activation.

Further support for the idea that expansion and diversification occur after the initial period comes from the *number* of activity areas in the initial and succeeding periods. In Atlanta, 49% of the attributed elite were initiated *via* a single sphere of activity; Raleigh influentials ranked lower with 37%. Taking these two groups and examining their responses for all the time periods, we find that, almost without exception, the actors widen their areas of activity. Do they achieve the same scopes as those individuals who began with more than one activity area? On the whole, they do not. In Atlanta, those initiated *via* a single sphere have an average of three areas for all time periods, while those initiated *via* two or more areas average 3.6 areas. In Raleigh, the corresponding figures are 3.2 and 4.3, a much more significant ratio. Actors who are introduced *via* two or more types of activity are also more likely to achieve greater diversification over an extended period of time.

Even though a centrifugal tendency exists among the attributed influentials in both communities, it may be that a centripetal force works to restrict the *major* spheres of action. To explore this possibility, we classified as *major* activity areas each one that accounted for at least 25% of all those mentioned by each respondent. The 25% figure is admittedly arbitrary. Given the diverse natures of the activities listed, however, any higher figure would probably make it difficult to establish major activity areas at all, while lower figures would produce too many major emphases for meaningful analysis.

In the light of prior rankings, the distribution in Table 27 is not unexpected. As before, the three leading areas are government affairs, welfare drives, and civic organizations. Only about one-tenth of the respondents in each community had none of these three as a major sphere. Furthermore, 43% in each community listed some combination of the three spheres as major activities. That is, two of the three constituted one-half or more of the major types of activity listed by 43% of the actors. In addition to highlighting the major avenues of influence, the figures suggest that participation in these three spheres is highly associated with reputations for influence. The figures also belie the notion that leadership or prestige in cultural, "society," entertainment, religious, business, or professional affairs is enough, by itself, to earn the individual high political status.

So far, we have sketched the relative importance of various activities for inaugurating and perpetuating influence roles— the avenues of career development. From some of the data, we

Table 27. Major Activity Areas for Attributed Influentials in Two Communities over Extended Length of Time, by Rank and Percentage

	ATLANTA		RALEIGH	
	Rank	Per cent*	Rank	Per cent
Government affairs	1	53	2	43
Welfare drives	2	47	1	49
Civic organizations	3	35	3	37
Electoral	4	18	6	11
Social-cultural	5.5	12	7.5	3
Professional organizations	5.5	12	9	0
Educational	7	8	7.5	3
Religious	8.5	2	5	14
Service clubs	8.5	2	4	17
Number		(49)		(35)

*Percentages do not total 100% because most actors mentioned more than one activity.

can infer certain conclusions about the usual types of progression found. For example, people tend to expand from their initiatory roles into other spheres, while at the time developing major interests. We shall now examine a more specific indicator of career development at the community level.

Do actors tend to remain in the same activity spheres in which they are initiated, or do they, in their subsequent diversification, drop them in favor of major roles in other areas? One plausible hypothesis is that, if the initial activity is in one of the prime areas for gaining and exercising influence, then the individual will remain in that area although he may also expand to others. Conversely, if the initial endeavor is in an area of minor specialization, then the individual will drop it as a major part of his repertory.

To test this hypothesis, we distributed the responses according to major or minor types of initial activity. The major types included civic groups, welfare drives, and public affairs; the minor types consisted of religious, electoral, service-club, professional-organization, educational, and social-cultural activities.

The data support the hypothesis to a marked degree. Eighty-two per cent of the Atlanta attributed influentials (N = 51) and 76% of their Raleigh counterparts (N = 38) who had major types of initial activities continued them into later periods. In contrast, only 39% of the Atlanta respondents (N = 31) and 25% of those in Raleigh (N = 28) who had minor initial activities continued them as major roles. If an individual is initiated in one of the major arenas, he clearly is inclined to use that arena as a major avenue of influence.

Because those actors initiated *via* minor activities tend to drop them, it is clear that these roles serve primarily as stepping stones to other, more important roles. The actors do not necessarily drop these lesser varieties completely, but they take on new roles to supplement and supplant them. These new roles usually involve the main activity areas in community affairs—welfare drives, government affairs, and civic-organization work.

This wholesale transition does not imply particular motives among the actors. It may be that some men consciously enter into leadership in service clubs, church organizations, cultural activities, and so forth, with an eye to ultimate entrance into other realms. It may also be that they find themselves swept along with little conscious direction. Although the data do not tell what, if any, deliberate strategies are involved, they do make clear that certain types of initiatory roles remain highly salient to the actors and the community while other types do not.

Intergenerational Political Socialization

This chapter began by examining the importance of political socialization in the childhoods of today's actors in the community. Political socialization, in terms of father's level of activity in community affairs, did not appear to be significantly related to present levels of status in community decision-making and of political behavior. Nevertheless, we cannot say, in cases where the father's involvement in community issues was high, that it did not have an effect on the son at a later point in time. It is, therefore, of more than passing interest to discover if today's community influentials are socializing their sons toward high involvement. This problem is all the more compelling in view of the traditions of inherited community leadership that are undoubtedly strong in some communities. Neither Atlanta nor Raleigh have strong family dynasties, however.

All the respondents were asked in the formal interviews if they had any adult sons, and if these sons were active in community affairs. Among those with adult sons, there is a tendency for the sons to be active in community affairs.[12] This tendency applies to about 80% of the attributed influentials in each community and of the prescribed influentials in Atlanta. One clear exception is the prescribed influentials in Raleigh, whose sons are primarily inactive. The small number of prescribed influentials with adult sons (eight) renders this finding inconclusive, however.

On the other hand, in the groups with active sons, the data support the notion that active fathers tend to encourage active sons. Occasionally, this encouragement takes the form of the son's entrance into the father's firm, with resulting freedom from some of the insecurity that might inhibit the young man who must still establish himself. In Atlanta, for example, one elderly influential has a son in his law firm; the son is slowly edging into the higher levels of community decision-making. In Raleigh, the son of a wealthy supply-company president encounters few obstacles in becoming activated.

Not all the active sons live in the home communities of their fathers. When they do not, their activation results in no net gain for intergenerational leadership within the community. About 70% of the active sons of attributed influentials in Atlanta (N=14) and Raleigh (N=12) and 60% of the active sons of prescribed influentials in Atlanta (N=14) do remain in their parents' communities, however.

Is there any relationship between having had an active father and having an active son? Do today's influentials who had active fathers socialize their own sons to a greater extent than do those who did not have active fathers? The data present no conclusive evidence on this point, but in Atlanta a very slight indication exists that sons of active fathers are more likely to produce active sons than are the sons of inactive fathers (77% *versus* 65% with Ns of 22 and 17). Raleigh influentials, however, differ little on this point, with approximately two-thirds of the offspring of both active (N = 22) and inactive (N = 6) fathers having active sons. The small number with inactive fathers makes generalization highly dubious.

Our findings on political socialization lend only slight support to the idea that the family is a dominant factor in transmitting and implanting predispositions toward more highly politicized behavior in the community. To be sure, we are working with elites. Findings like those summarized by Hyman[13] are drawn primarily from cross-sections of large populations and demonstrate the strong influence of the family on both orientation and participation of the future adult. It may be that, if we had reached further down in the decision-making structure, our findings would have coincided with the larger studies. Nevertheless, the fact that these elites do deviate from normal patterns suggests that the proclivity for exercising influence in community decision-making, as a specialized type of political behavior, is not dependent upon political socializing factors of the home. These may guide the individual, but they are not necessarily determinative. The implications of our findings for students and practitioners of community decision-making is that the intergenerational transfer of politically oriented behavior is not assured and, therefore, not a certain source of community leadership.

When factors other than the home and the family are considered as socializing forces, the data reveal that the individual is most likely to be drawn into participation through friends or associates. Recruitment from governmental sources appeared to be more important for the first-level attributed influentials and government officials than for the other status-groups. As far as initiatory activities were concerned, welfare drives, government affairs, and participation in civic organizations were most important for the attributed influentials. These arenas remained the most important for them in later activities, as well. The findings also highlight the pre-eminence of the governmental-political arena in the acquisition and maintenance of political roles and status.

Comparative materials from a study of four state legislatures and from another community suggest that status- and role-acquisition varies according to the kind of actor and political system. State legislators appear to be more influenced by their families and their own personal motivations than do the community influentials. Furthermore, even though the attributed influentials of Atlanta and Raleigh use civic organizations, welfare drives, and government affairs as leading avenues to influence roles, persistent variations occur between the two communities. Atlanta influentials also employ the minor avenue of professional organizations, while Raleigh influentials emphasize service clubs and religious activities as vehicles for decision-making roles.

NOTES

1. Herbert Hyman, *Political Socialization: A Study in the Psychology of Political Behavior* (New York: The Free Press of Glencoe, 1959). Since Hyman's survey, a number of provocative studies have been undertaken. See particularly Robert D. Hess and David Easton. "The Child's Changing Image of the President," *Public Opinion Quarterly*, XXIV (Winter, 1960) 632-44; and Fred I. Greenstein, "More on Children's Images of the President," *Public Opinion Quarterly*, XXV (Winter, 1961), 648-54.

2. Talcott Parsons, *The Social System* (New York: The Free Press of Glencoe, 1951), pp. 207-8.

3. Hyman suggests that we must know the total family structure, politically speaking, in order to assess adequately the political socialization of the child. For the type of behavior with which we are dealing, however, most participation comes from the masculine rather than the feminine side of the family.

4. Most of the Raleigh study was conducted by the author in the summer of 1959. This investigation did not go so deeply into the processes of community decision-making as did the Atlanta research.

5. This comparison extends to the total group of status-holders in each community. In Atlanta, 51% of the natives reported that their fathers were highly active, while in Raleigh, 74% reported the same.

6. Not unexpectedly, father's occupation is related to his reported community-activity level. In Atlanta, only 15% of the active fathers, compared to 40% of the inactive fathers, had low-status occupations. Raleigh data, though still in the same direction, show corresponding percentages of only 10% and 22%.

7. Nor is it anomalous to find that in Raleigh the naming of family members was double that of Atlanta, although it is still a rather small proportion.

8. Heinz Eulau, *et al.*, "The Political Socialization of American State Legislators," in Eulau, *et al.*, eds., *Legislative Behavior: A Reader in Theory and Research* (New York: The Free Press of Glencoe, 1959), pp. 305-13. Legislators in California, New Jersey, Ohio, and Tennessee comprised the subjects of the study.

9. An open-ended question was used in both the legislative and the two community studies. Eulau and his associates asked, "How did you become interested in politics? What is your earliest recollection of being interested in it?" (*Ibid.*, p. 312, n. 4). In Table 24, we made the following changes in category headings to conform with the legislative study. Relatives and friends and associates are classified as "primary groups"; special drives and organizational membership or office-holding as "participation"; occupa-

tional position and gradual entrance as "events or conditions"; personal predisposition as "predisposition and beliefs."

10. There is some danger in using 1936 as the first possible year, given the advanced ages of a few of the respondents who may well have been active before this period. The danger has been minimized by the fact that many of the respondents had moved to the respective cities since 1936, that 1936 actually did mark the first period of activity for many of the younger and middle-aged respondents, and that the types of activity designated are quite similar to those of younger people.

11. A preliminary decision-making analysis by this writer of Charlotte, North Carolina, a city of approximately 130,000, suggests that church leadership is one well established funnel to community leadership. Most of the so-called leaders of the community had served apprenticeships as church leaders, and some were still church leaders. Most of the top influentials took part in promoting a Billy Graham revival, an activity difficult to imagine in Atlanta and only slightly more conceivable in Raleigh.

12. The number of actors with adult sons is eighteen each for the attributed and prescribed influentials in Atlanta, fifteen for attributed influentials and eight for prescribed influentials in Raleigh. Too few economic dominants had adult sons to provide meaningful data.

13. Hyman, *op. cit.*, pp. 69-87.

CONCLUSIONS

We have compared three major status-groups or elites in Atlanta, primarily on the basis of their roles in community decision-making. In the process, some insight has also been gained
into the decision-making structure of the community. The analysis can also be viewed from the perspective of the major scholarly
approaches to community decision-making studies outlined in
Chapter 1. An interpretive summary of the findings follows.

Status and Role Relationships

Our central objective was to examine the relationship between an actor's political status and his political roles—or behavior—in community decision-making. More specifically, we
asked whether those in different political status-groups perform
similar, dissimilar, or mixed roles? The major groups were the
attributed influentials, both first and second echelons; the prescribed influentials, both government officials and civic-staff
personnel; and the economic dominants.

Economic Dominants. We should remember that those we
have labeled economic dominants are "pure" types; that is, they
are not perceived as influentials. Such pure types composed a

distinct majority of *all* economic notables in the study. In terms of social characteristics associated with political status, the economic dominants were the most heterogeneous of the three groups. This heterogeneity was especially true of their social backgrounds, which ranged from elite to very modest. Although all presently enjoy high socio-economic status, their cultural and intellectual endeavors are limited. A larger number of them than of the other groups are "self-made" men, which partially explains their reluctance to participate in community policy-making. Most of them are engaged in manufacturing enterprises. At least half the economic dominants do not have strong roots in the community—they were not born there, have not lived there so long as have the other actors, were not educated there, and conform least of all the actors to the city's dominant religious and partisan patterns. The combined social characteristics of the economic dominants are thus quite different from those of the other two elites.

Turning to actual forms of politicized behavior in the community, we found obvious reasons why the economic dominants are not perceived as influentials. Especially in comparison with the other two groups, the economic dominants are, for the most part, lowly politicized individuals. Of the major forms of politicized behavior studied—participation in organizations, interpersonal communication with significant actors, advice-giving, and levels of involvement in specific issues—only on the first did the economic dominants compare favorably with the other elites.

Information on the scope of their involvement in community issues and arenas reinforces the picture of the economic dominants as minor decision-makers. Regardless of the measure used for role-scopes, the economic dominants consistently scored lowest among the three major groupings.

Our data on decision-making roles and forms of power in the case studies offer probably the most vivid demonstration of the relative lack of power (though not necessarily of potential power) these economic notables exert in Atlanta. In our chronicling of the roles of key actors in the resolution of five issues, not one "pure" economic dominant appeared. Even their reported behavior from the questionnaire data indicates at best minimal or uncostly participation.

As we have noted, these pure economic dominants constituted a majority of the economic notables studied. Even if
we consider the fifteen economic giants who are also perceived
influentials, however, there is little basis for characterizing Atlanta as a community ruled by a tight-knit group of economic
notables.

Prescribed influentials. The social backgrounds and characteristics of these actors are middle-class. Most come from moderately successful families, have had at least some college
education, and earn higher than average incomes. Many have
migrated to Atlanta. Their attendance at middle-class Protestant
churches, their greater allegiance to the Democratic party, and
their reading habits help to identify the government officials as
the most locally oriented elite. Occupationally, the prescribed
influentials are composed of a strong core of professionals with
a sprinkling from other vocations.

The prescribed influentials are, for the most part, quite
politicized in their community roles. Within this elite, the
government officials have higher rates of interaction with government officials and representative leaders in the community,
are more prolific advice-givers in substantive areas, and usually
more involved in community issues than are the civic staffers.
Civic-staff personnel, on the other hand, are more active in
local organizations, their natural habitat.

The prescribed influentials, especially the government officials, have high scopes of involvement and high performance of
deliberate power acts in many substantive arenas and specific
issues. While government officials concentrate most of their
activities in the government arena, the civic staffers also participate in fund-raising and private endeavors. The fairly extensive
scopes of the prescribed influentials suggest that their official
positions permit some of them, at any rate, to engage in a great
range of public "games" and issues.

As for their decision-making behavior in specific issues, the
prescribed influentials play a diversity of roles. In the bond
program, for example, some of them performed initiatory activities, help set priorities, engaged in promotional activities, and
assisted in implementation. Their ability to use filter power to
help determine outcomes was particularly evident in this issue.
These activities were carried out in co-operation with attributed

influentials, as well as with other prescribed influentials, so that inter-status relationships were apparent.

Although they do engage in a number of decision-making roles, the prescribed influentials are generally less pivotal than the attributed elite in the allocation of values. Many of them do vitally affect these allocations, and some even formally pass on them, but when real controversy has been aroused, the prescribed influentials by themselves do not have the resources to determine the course of events. On the other hand, this stage is by no means always the most important in the decision-making continuum, and proximate causation is at best difficult to isolate in decision-making. At any rate, the case studies demonstrate that the prescribed influentials can exercise power and do play decisive roles in deciding community issues. Their roles are consistent with their status.

Attributed influentials. In many ways, the attributed influentials are the most empirically interesting status-group. For the "pure" economic dominants, we could expect a congruence between their political status, which did not suggest highly politicized roles, and their actual roles. We could also predict that, because of their positions, the prescribed influentials would be highly politicized, although the dimensions and nuances of their roles remained to be explored. But the attributed influentials presented the greatest test of the hypothesized positive association between status and role. Although being perceived as influentials warranted their classification as occupants of an elite political status, there was no guarantee that they were actually performing determinative roles in Atlanta's power structure. It remained to determine empirically whether political status was actually matched by role-behavior.[1]

A moderate degree of homogeneity in social characteristics and high social status were, of course, to be expected. In fact, the attributed influentials stand out as having the most privileged social backgrounds, as having had at least some college education, and as enjoying high socio-economic status in the community. Of all the groups, they have the closest attachments to Atlanta in terms of birth site, place of rearing, length of residence in the community, and place of education. Occupationally, they represent a diverse number of economic enterprises with no one type predominating. The attributed influentials are the most cosmopolitan of the elites, despite their apparent closer attachments to home.

More than the other elites, they demonstrate the overlapping of the heights of the political-status and social-status systems. Certain social features may be termed prerequisites for achieving the political status of an attributed influential. We have demonstrated, however, that holding a major economic or governmental post is neither a prerequisite nor a guarantee of attributed status. Those who were economic dominants as well as perceived influentials came mainly from nonmanufacturing firms, which are located in the central business district, are locally owned, and have their locus of consumption in the immediate metropolitan area. The government officials located at the top of the two status systems are also of a special kind—primarily nonprofessional and elective.

The similarity in their social characteristics did not necessarily mean that the reputed elite would exhibit role-behaviors symbolic of political influentials. Yet, according to the gross measurements of politicization, they are as highly politicized as the prescribed influentials and far more so than the economic dominants. Surprisingly, one of the ways in which they are most politicized is in the holding of public office, both past and present—"surprisingly" because much discussion of reputational leaders of a community treats them as "powers behind the throne" who do not become overtly involved in governmental affairs.

Top-level attributed influentials outranked their second-level counterparts on most forms of politicized role-playing in community decision-making. This finding is significant because it suggests that perceptions of power are directly or indirectly linked with overt forms of politically oriented behavior. According to the indices of politicization, the upper-level attributed influentials are the most politicized group in the study, although the government officials are a close second in many instances. Like the prescribed influentials, the attributed elite must be termed highly politicized.

One of the most intriguing aspects is role-scope. Most attributed influentials included the governmental arena (generally the most rewarding decision-making arena) among major recent activities. A solid majority named issues of major importance

to the community as those in which they had performed significant activities. In scope of specific endeavors within the governmental sphere, the first-level influentials again outranked their
second-level colleagues, as well as the other groups. Like the prescribed influentials, most of the perceived elite are polymorphic
activists, though some included more arenas than did others.
Holding governmental positions was found to be highly associated with extensive role-scopes. While only a minority exercise
widely generalized power, only a handful were restricted to one
issue-area.

An even more revealing measure of the positive association
between reputed influence and performance of decision-making
roles was provided by the case studies, in which the attributed
influentials played key roles in the decision-making process and
exercised forms of power in the community. In all five issues
examined, a significant number of the key actors were attributed
influentials, although they by no means dominated the ranks
of key actors. Like the prescribed influentials, the attributed
elite can be found playing any of the five key roles suggested.
In the mayoralty election, for example, they performed roles
of initiation, allocation of values, and promotion. They played
some of their roles almost entirely by themselves (as in the "top
leaders" meeting); in others, they co-operated with prescribed
influentials (as in the informal conclaves during the urban
renewal-public housing conflict). Like the prescribed elite, then,
the reputed influentials perform roles in accordance with their
status.

The data on status and role acquisition are most complete
for the attributed influentials. Their tendency to have had
fathers active in community affairs is not strong, but they themselves are attracted to and are induced to participate in community decision-making. Friends and associates are the most
compelling recruiting forces, with occupational position, drives
and campaigns, and organizations next. A substantial share of
these forces originate in the governmental arena.

Welfare drives, government affairs, and civic organizations
are the prime initial avenues to issue-involvement, and professional organizations are an important minor one. The three
avenues tend to remain the prime areas for exercising power
in the community and thus for perpetuating the status of attributed influentials. Although they do tend to socialize their sons

toward community participation, intergenerational political socialization apparently does not provide a strong source of continuing community leadership.

The Power Structure

Although the primary purpose of this study was to investigate systematically the social components and political role correlates of political status, we also anticipated that some tentative conclusions might be reached about the upper echelons of the power structure of Atlanta. Such conclusions do emerge from data on general politicization, the extent of role-scopes, the case studies, and exercise of power on multiple issues. No pretense can be made of describing the complete power structure, since we have limited the study to certain elites within that structure. The evidence does suggest, however, that the attributed and prescribed influentials are not only highly politicized but are also central actors in a number of substantive arenas and specific issues. There is, then, a reliable basis for a few general statements about the power structure and the general decision-making process in Atlanta.

One point is that these central decision-makers are not uniformly drawn from the ranks of those with the highest economic status. In fact, the "pure" economic dominants were almost uniformly lowly politicized and only slightly involved in significant issues in the community. This evidence should effectively dispel the notion that economic position is invariantly correlated with political power in Atlanta. At the same time, some economic notables are quite influential. To put it another way, ranking economic position is only one of a number of factors related to political power and, by itself, is unlikely to be the decisive factor.

A second point is that those who are perceived to be most influential in the community and those who hold positions of prescribed influence do engage in role-activities that stamp them as influential in resolving issues.

A subsidiary point arises here. Power and influence do not rest solely in the hands of the "big mules" (generally the first-level perceived influentials). Those in the top reputed elite are not the only significant actors in decision-making. Rather, as the material on role-behavior in general and decision-making performance on specific issues illustrates, the prescribed influentials and secondary attributed influentials also play key roles in issue resolution. Depending on what roles are regarded as the most significant in the decision-making continuum, either the attributed or the prescribed influentials may exert the "most" important influence. Despite a general tendency for the elites to become activated at different points in the continuum and to exert different forms of power (positive, veto, and filter), it is difficult to assign firm priorities of importance to their differential roles.[2] Both influential types may also perform similar roles and exercise similar types of power on a given issue.

A third point is that, although a homogeneous elite does not rule Atlanta, a coalition of actors, organizations, and institutions does tend to prevail in most important community issues. The main components of this coalition are the business-civic, the governmental-political, and the older Negro leadership. Particular elements and actors in the coalition may vary from issue to issue. Open, heated conflict among these forces seldom arises, although milder forms of competition do occur. Accommodations among these components, rather than struggle, is the rule. On the one issue in this study in which the coalition suffered a setback, the tangible outcome (650 of a desired 1000 units of public housing) still represented a major victory over opponents to public housing and urban renewal. The coalition is not always complete, of course. It was most complete on the omnibus bond program, least united on the public housing-urban renewal issue. But the important point to note is that there do appear to be coalitions, rather than a single, homogeneous agent or group of actors who unilaterally decide what will "go" and what will not "go" in Atlanta. In the exercise of veto power, however, one or two elements of the coalition may effectively prevent a change in the *status quo,* as they did in the fluoridation and Community Chest issues. It is also possible that the larger coalition may be undergoing change, as some of the older political leaders lose power and as social changes alter the metropolis.

Although it is true that a coalition composed of attributed and prescribed influentials and the institutions they represent frequently determines outcomes in Atlanta, it is also true that different institutions and different actors may play determinative roles in the various substructures of power. Only a few of the actors actually participated (to omit the question of influence itself) in even a majority of the substantive arenas and specific issues surveyed. Even for those actors who do show wide-ranging influence and participation, the evidence is not convincing that they have unilaterally achieved desired outcomes. They have, rather, acted as part of one coalition or another.[3]

If the power structure is not monolithic, neither is it amorphous. Many actors do participate and exert influence in several arenas, and generally similar processes mark their activities. Certain repeated personal interactions do occur, certain actors traditionally make major decisions in particular substantive areas, certain means of access to governmental and private officials are employed time and again, and certain "ways of getting things done" are used repeatedly. In essence, then, the structure is neither so monolithic as Hunter claims in his earlier work on Atlanta nor so fragmented as some other metropolises appear to be.[4]

Integration of Other Approaches

In our opening chapter, various approaches to the study of community decision-making were noted. We declared that this study would be eclectic and would borrow elements from all the approaches cited. It may be that the study has also contributed something to these other approaches. We shall briefly examine how the approaches were used and what light, if any, is shed on them as a result of our study.

The orientation of traditional political science was described as too narrow and formalistic for an adequate understanding of community decision-making. Yet it does draw the researcher's attention to the central prescribed functions of governmental institutions in our society. On the basis of our study, emphasis upon government officials and institutions seems well grounded. Should this claim sound like a truism, the reader need only refer to various community studies noted in Chapter 1 that view governmental institutions and officials as derivative of and subordinate to economic and social institutions.

It is not merely that the most significant community decisions are made in Atlanta's governmental arena. More revealing are the high incidence of governmental office holders among the reputed influentials, the high participation of local government officials in interpersonal relationships with community influentials, the exercise of power by government officials in specific issues, and the extensive role-scopes of many governmental office holders. Although there was sufficient evidence of political actors working through or upon government officials to achieve their ends, there was little to indicate that either elective or appointive officials, professional or nonprofessional, were merely subject to the desires of big businessmen, party politicians, minority groups, and others.

The contribution of this study to traditional political science rests in placing governmental institutions and processes within the framework of other institutions and processes in the community. This configuration is not unfamiliar at the national level, but has usually been overlooked at the local level. The intertwining of the governmental sphere with economic, social, civic, cultural, racial, and other spheres has been implicitly and at times explicitly acknowledged in our work. One new tack open to research on community decision-making thus lies in the direction of more "governmental process" studies, similar to those at the national and, to a lesser extent, state levels.

Traditional sociology, with its emphasis on social stratification and its consequences for decision-making, is the second approach described in Chapter 1. Although this orientation seemed too broad for community decision-making analysis, it did promise usefulness as a sensitizer to aspects of the political process that are often overlooked. Indeed, the major concepts—political statuses and political roles—were derived from social-stratification and structure theory. This approach also led us to consideration of the social backgrounds and present social characteristics of the status-holders. The findings demonstrate that certain clusters of social features, both present and past, tend to differentiate the status-groups. The impact of social processes and social structure was also discussed in terms of political socialization.

At other points in the text, the importance of social structure and social stratification has been alluded to, although not always in precise terms. For example, the urban-renewal chairman's inability to converse easily with many of the attributed influentials was primarily a function of social-status differentiation. We also pointed out that high social status is usually a prerequisite for lay directorship of virtually any governmental or fund-raising enterprise (although high status alone is not sufficient).

Probably the greatest contribution of our research to traditional community sociology lies in its tempering effect on social-stratification theory. We have demonstrated that socio-economic status is not an infallible guide to political status or to political power and influence. Many of the works by traditional sociologists seem to equate economic and social position with political power and status.[5] Such equivalence is absent in Atlanta. To be sure, the influentials do come from the middle and upper strata, but within these strata vast differences exist.

A third orientation was also described—interpersonal influence. Even though this approach is at once too narrow and too broad for maximum utility, it too proved helpful. Most of our references to interpersonal influence were implicit, rather than explicit. In giving advice on matters of concern to the community, the attributed and prescribed influentials clearly engaged in behavior associated with interpersonal influence—and much more than did the economic dominants. Similar behavior was apparent with respect to various government officials and group leaders.

More direct evidence of interpersonal influence came in the case studies. The Community Chest officials' ability to persuade a United States senator to help in vetoing an attempt to exclude the Urban League from the Chest drive is a good example of interpersonal influence. The recommendations of civic-staff and second-level influentials to a cluster of "top" influentials on the mayoralty election are another vivid demonstration of the use of interpersonal influence. Filter power, as exercised in these cases, particularly lends itself to the interpersonal-influence approach. Certain actors, especially those in staff capacities, are able to wield a great deal of interpersonal influence because of their recognized expertise.

If this study has contributed any insight on the place of interpersonal influence in community decision-making, it is probably the suggestion that such transactions occur across various status-groupings. While it may be true that communication with one's own peers is quite important for decision-making at the level of the individual voter, it need not follow that the same is true in community decision-making. Interpersonal influentials need not be personal friends, as is usual among those who influence voting behavior. They resemble instead actors in most organized enterprises where people attempt interpersonal influence because of the demands of the situation. Tapping the horizontal and vertical flows of interpersonal influence is an important area of research in community decision-making.

Case studies were central to our efforts to relate political statuses and roles. In the introductory remarks about case studies in community decision-making analysis, we made the point that their usefulness is limited by the unique qualities of each case. In an attempt to overcome this difficulty, we included five cases, describing three of them in depth. Our purpose was to ascertain how statuses and roles are related within the framework of live issues. A paradigm of decision-making and distinction among three types of power acts helped to carry the case studies beyond the level of pure narrative.

The case studies demonstrated that the two major influential elites—attributed and prescribed—merited their status designations to the extent that they were indeed the major actors in the issues surveyed. Without the case studies, this point would have been much more difficult, if not impossible, to establish. The advantage of analyzing several cases lies in the fact that the findings about power and process cannot be attributed merely to the unique features of a particular case. For isolating the major actors and determining the elements of process, the use of the multiple case-study approach proved invaluable.

Integrating fairly detailed case-study material with structured interview data was not particularly difficult. In fact, from the experience of this study, it seems a fruitful way to proceed in community decision-making research. Case studies add substance to the framework of descriptive and analytical behavioral categories. By the same token, applying analytical constructs to the case-study material heightens its value.

Power-structure studies were initially described as those that seek to portray the general configuration of power or decision-making in the community. It is a more general approach and, hopefully, more conducive to generalization. By restricting our research to select political actors and to the range of questions pursued, we attempted to portray some of the major actors and processes of decision-making in Atlanta. Without a general orientation to the power structure, we would not have been able to treat so wide a range of phenomena. Nor could we have attempted to relate roles and statuses to the general pattern of decision-making.

We did not so much attempt to describe the structure of power in Atlanta as to describe the behavior of certain actors within that structure, but without concern for various arenas of decision-making, various modes of power, and various types of politicized behavior, such an effort would have faltered. The power-structure orientation broadened the scope of the study to include sufficient phenomena to designate fairly clearly the major actors and institutions within the power structure.

Our study suggests in turn that power-structure inquiries may benefit from a variety of approaches, conceptual schemes, and research strategies. The use of concepts like status-groups, role-activities, politicization, forms of power, components of decision-making, role-scopes, and status and role acquisition is, of course, only one of many ways to study community decision-making within the perspective of the power structure. The combination of all these varied concepts, however, plus a number of research techniques and forms of exposition, indicates that catholicity is possible and rewarding.

NOTES

1. Technically this statement does not apply to the fifteen government officials who also met the criteria for perceived influentials. There is, however, the possibility that they, like some economic dominants, would be perceived as influential only because of their positions.

2. This point is essentially the same as that made by Roscoe C. Martin, Frank J. Munger, et al., *Decisions in Syracuse* (Bloomington: Indiana University Press, 1961), pp. 311-21. "The 'powerful' community leader without idea men to suggest possibilities to him, or experts to package his program, or publicists to put wheels under it, or brokers to facilitate its consideration, or transmitters to bring it before the nominal decision-makers, can do little with his power. Community power is a network of action, not a locus of residence." (p. 319.)

3. Little attention has been devoted to forms of unintended influence. This phenomenon cannot be overestimated as a significant element in the decision-making structure of a community. Data gathered rather casually in Atlanta indicate that the prescribed and attributed influentials unintentionally influence many decisions by the very fact that their anticipated reactions figure prominently in the decision-making of other actors. It seems

that prescribed influentials, since they are often in subordinate hierarchical positions, more often anticipate the reactions of attributed influentials than the reverse. Because the analysis in this work has been based primarily on overt behavior, our sketch of the power structure is incomplete. See Peter B. Clark, "Civic Leadership: The Symbols of Legitimacy," (paper delivered at the 1960 meeting of the American Political Science Association, New York, September, 1960), for an excellent discussion of the anticipated influence of big businessmen in community decision-making.

4. Some critics of Hunter have tended, implicitly or explicitly, to reject any model of a community's power structure other than that of a competitive pluralistic structure with governmental and political leaders providing what cohesive direction may exist. In a brilliant review of Robert A. Dahl's *Who Governs?* (New Haven: Yale University Press, 1961), H. D. Price questions the general, uncritical application of the New Haven model to other communities. See *Yale Law Journal,* LXXI (July, 1962), pp. 1589-96.

5. For amplification of this point, see Nelson Polsby, *Community Power and Political Theory* (New Haven: Yale University Press, 1963).

INDEX